Unsung Heroes

of Wilkes County, Georgia

Volume 1

Edward M. Anderson, Sr.

Dr. Jackie S. Henderson
YOUR FAMILY RESEARCH & PUBLISHING
Stone Mountain, GA

DANBURG GRANITE MEMORIAL

IN MEMORY OF THE BLACK CITIZENS OF THE VILLAGE

Entrapped involuntarily in a system of servitude until 1865. They were thereafter entangled with the white citizens in a system of cotton-tenant-farming that exploited both through 1945 for the advantage of northern industrial capitalism. Both bondages were born by the black citizens with incredible fortitude, patience, and humor.

Omnia ad dei gloriam

ISBN-13:978-1492818533
ISBN-10:1492818534

DEDICATION

My wife, G. Kathryn Anderson;
and my parents,
Veola Cofer Anderson and the late
Leroy Anderson, Sr.

CONTENTS

ACKNOWLEDGEMENTS

To God be the Glory, great things God is doing in our lives. Great things God has done in the lives of all those featured in this book. And great things God has done in the lives of all those who supported me in any small way, over the years, as I have written the articles that are compiled in this book.

I am most grateful to my wife, Kathryn for her love, encouragement, confidence in me, understanding, proofreading and typing skills, and extraordinary organizational and clerical ability throughout this endeavor.

I thank my 92 year old mother, Veola Cofer Anderson for instilling in me and all of her children an appreciation, love, and respect for God, family, church, community, country, and especially for Wilkes County and its people. I thank my late father, Leroy Anderson, Sr. for instilling in me a strong work ethic, and a sense of duty and honor to family and community. He taught me that "you can do anything you set your mind to do."

I thank my late grandparents, Deacon Charlie & Sister Hattie Willis Cofer and Deacon Roy & Sister Ethel Willis Anderson, for their Christian example, and for nurturing and answering my many questions from the time of my childhood, regarding some of the unsung heroes of their generation and earlier.

I thank four of my favorite people for their inspiration: Amirah, Elijah, Josiah and Selah.

I thank television news anchor, Chris Clackum who, in 1981, did a feature story on my parents for the local Charlotte, NC television station and called it "Unsung Heroes." This ignited in me a desire to establish a ministry to uplift the lives of hardworking, ordinary people by telling their story and naming them as "Unsung Heroes."

I thank Washington News-Reporter Editor, Parks "Sparky" Newsome for his willingness to edit and publish the articles I submitted to him in the "Unsung Heroes of Wilkes County" series during Black History Month for each of the past several years.

I thank the late Dr. Charles D. Saggus, Walter Lee Currie and other grandsons of Walter Lee Sutton for the inspiration provided through the Danburg Granite Monument they erected.

I thank the late Leola Young, Joe Anderson, Ethel Person, Gladys Nelson, Elnora Anderson, Mary Gatling, Leroy Anderson Jr., Rev. Paul Anderson, Steve Blackmon, Rev. Kenneth Walker, the late Rev. G. L. Avery, the late Rev. Robert L. Walton, the late Rev. Albert Rucker, Jr., the late Ted Bush, and many others for their inspiration and regular, positive, and encouraging critique of my "Unsung Heroes" articles.

I thank the following people for their interviews which allowed me to tell their stories and /or the stories of their loved ones: the late Rev Albert Zellars, Deacon Albert Rucker, Sr., Gartrell Robinson, Jr., Veola Cofer Anderson, the late Bessie Wellmaker McLendon, Warden Willie C. Bolton, William James Willis, Sr., the late Oree Dee Willis, Rev. Kenneth Walker, CSM Samuel Edward "Ed' Jenkins, Rev & Mrs. Henry M. Easley, Deacon & Mrs. D. W. Dunn, Dea. Joe L. Anderson, Sr., and Arthur Watson "Doc" Danner.

I thank the late Mrs. Doris Booker for having kept the thirst for knowledge of Black History alive among the citizens of Wilkes County for decades through her annual Black History Programs.

I thank Paula & Tommie Broadnax for their friendship and inspiration as Paula recently completed her first book.

INTRODUCTION

From the earliest days in Wilkes County, Georgia, there have been free and enslaved men and women of color, some nameless, who have sacrificed, labored, bled, and even died for the freedom, growth, and development of Wilkes County, Georgia. This book is a compilation of writings prepared over a period of eight years, designed to inform the reader of the superb contributions of some of these great "Unsung Heroes."

Several years ago, the village of Danburg and the memory of the late Walter Lee Sutton (1863-1947) were honored by Sutton's grandsons, WLC, JSS, CES, Jr. and Dr. Charles D. Saggus with the construction of a gigantic granite memorial which stands on the corner of Bradford Road and Highway 44, in Danburg, GA. The granite memorial appears on the front of this book. Danburg is the home community of the businessman and merchant, Walter Lee Sutton and his family.

On one side of the monument reads the inscription ***"In honor of the black citizens of the village -- Entrapped involuntarily in a system of servitude until 1865, they were thereafter entangled with the white citizens in a system of cotton-tenant-farming that exploited both through 1945 for the advantage of northern industrial capitalism. Both bondages were born by the black citizens with incredible fortitude, patience and humor. – Omnia Ad Dei Gloriam"***

The inscription is applicable beyond the Danburg community. In fact, it is equally true throughout Wilkes County, the State of Georgia, and the entire south. Nevertheless, the labor, craftsmanship, service, and ingenuity of people of color have been essential to the growth and development of the county and state.

In his 1996 book entitled, *AGRARIAN ARCADIA - Anglo Virginian Planters of Wilkes County, Georgia*, Dr. Charles D. Saggus points out that in the February 5, 1777 Constitution for the State of Georgia, Wilkes County is one of the original counties in Georgia. He states that "When it was created, it included most of the hinterland north of Augusta." Enslaved people of color were the primary artisans and "hewers of the wood and drawers of the water" that changed the hinterlands to farms, churches, villages, and cities. In a real sense, they are unsung heroes.

In his book entitled, *THE HISTORY OF WILKES COUNTY, GEORGIA,* Robert M. "Skeet" Willingham points out in his very first chapter that two free men of color (Gideon and Matthew Cheivers) were among the 23 men who received warrants for survey along the Savannah and Broad Rivers and Fishing and Pistol Creeks from 1758 to 1768. This, of course, occurred prior to the 1773 ceding of hundreds of thousands of acres by the Native Americans (who had inhabited the entire area for thousands of years) to the British.

Willingham goes on to tell of a January 1774 skirmish which occurred when a ban of Creek Indians attacked a fort occupied by settlers, to include enslaved people of color. Seven of the settlers were killed. However, "the bravery of one of the Negroes in the fort aided the others in their defense. This courageous man rushed out of the blockhouse, grappled with one of the Indians, and shot him through the head."

Enslaved and free men of color were involved throughout the colonies in the building, maintenance and defense of their new homeland. On March 5, 1770, in the Boston Massacre, a free black man, Crispus Attucks was the first person to die for the freedom of America. James Neyland writes of Attucks in his 1995 book entitled, *Crispus Attucks, Patriot,* "He is one of the most important figures in African-American history, not for what he did for his own race but for what he did for all oppressed people everywhere. He is a reminder that the African American heritage is not only African, but American and it is a heritage that begins with the beginning of America."

Robert M. "Skeet" Willingham goes on to remind us of the 1779 sacrifice of another brave black Revolutionary War Patriot, Austin Dabney. He states, "One method by which a slave could earn his freedom, became apparent during the Revolutionary War. If the master did not wish to fight, a slave could be sent in his stead and thus gain his emancipation.

The best known slave who was freed by this method was Austin Dabney. He was a replacement soldier for his master, Richard Aycock, and was cited for gallantry at Kettle Creek where he aided Colonel Elijah Clark and was wounded by the Tories. He was cared for by the Harris family after his injury and out of gratitude began working for Harris. Dabney became quite attached to the Harris' son, William, and financed the young man's way through school and college. He also arranged for him to read law under Stephen Upson of Lexington in 1817.

William Harris became a prominent lawyer and distinguished jurist. Dabney acquired land in Madison County through the assistance of Upson and also received a government pension for his war-time service. Dabney was also a guest of General James Jackson, a longtime friend, at the mansion in Savannah when

Jackson was Governor of Georgia. Austin was perhaps the most outstanding example of the freed slave who, because of his character and service gained the highest respect and friendship of his white contemporaries." Austin Dabney is an authentic unsung hero of Wilkes County.

Michael Thurmond, in his 2003 book entitles *Freedom* states that Attorney William Harris would later name his son Austin Dabney Harris. Thurmond goes on to say that "Dabney's contributions to the war effort were singular, but by no means unique. Several other black men served with distinction as combat troops in the patriot army.

Nathan Fry joined Colonel Samuel Elbert's regiment at Savannah in 1775. Monday Floyd secured his freedom in 1782 by an act of the Georgia Assembly, which cited his heroic service during the war and directed the public treasury to pay Floyd's owner one hundred guineas for his manumission." There were many other similar instances throughout the colonies.

While the Declaration of Independence was signed on July 4, 1776, declaring the thirteen colonies to be free of British rule, the enslaved status of people of color did not change. The Constitution for the State of Georgia was adopted on February 5, 1777, declaring Georgia to be independent of the Crown of England, but this did not change the enslaved status of people of color, even though they had fought, bled and died for the freedom of Georgia and the colonies.

The blood, sweat, sacrifice, toils, and tears of enslaved artisans, soldiers, "hewers of the wood and drawers of the water", midwives, nannies, grannies, builders and farmers cry out for expressions of gratitude and respect for their unpaid and unquestionable contributions to the laying of the foundation for the

United States of America to become the greatest and most powerful nation in the history of the world. We can start by acknowledging what they did here, then accord them long overdue respect and honor, as did the grandsons of Walter Lee Sutton. For indeed, they are most deserving Unsung Heroes of Wilkes County, Georgia.

PART ONE

Religious Leaders

"But the fruit of the Spirit is love, joy, peace, patience, kindness, goodness, faithfulness, gentleness, self-control."

Galatians 5:23-24

"But those that wait on the Lord shall renew their strength; they shall mount up with wings like eagles, they shall run and not be weary, they shall walk and not faint."

Isaiah 40:31

"The church must be reminded that it is not the master or the servant of the state, but rather the conscience of the state. It must be the guide and the critic of the state, and never its tool. If the church does not recapture its prophetic zeal, it will become an irrelevant social club without moral or spiritual authority."

Martin Luther King, Jr.

Chapter 1

REV. LEWIS WILLIAMS

(1821-1906)

"A man of integrity and political savvy, as well as spiritual depth"

By 1893, he was regarded as "A man of integrity and political savvy, as well as spiritual depth, he had become one of the most respected individuals in the county" says Robert M. "Skeet" Willingham, Jr., in his 2002 book entitled *The History of Wilkes County, Georgia.*

Rev. Lewis Williams was first permitted to preach at First Baptist Church in Washington, GA in 1840. In 1867, he had asked the church to renew his preacher's license, for indeed, he was a pious preacher. In 1865, Eliza Frances "Fanny" Andrews, whose uncle owned Rev. Williams, had stated that he had been "an honored institution in the town."

In her 1995 Emory University Ph.D dissertation entitled "Before We Reach The Heavenly Fields: Religion and Society in Wilkes County, Georgia – 1783-1871," Jennifer Boone West states that Eliza Frances Andrews had regularly listened to Rev. Lewis Williams' prayers during family devotions at her uncle's home, and was brought up, in Fanny's words, "with as firm a belief in him as in the Bible itself."

West continues to quote Fanny Andrews, "When near death, her uncle had frequently sent for Lewis to talk and pray with him. Fanny Andrews even fondly remembered that she and the other children in her family had called him, not Lewis or 'Uncle Lewis' but simply 'Uncle' as though 'he had really been kin to them.'"

Within two years after the end of the Civil War, white people in the church and in the town were beginning to change their opinion about Rev. Williams. Fanny Andrews and others felt that he had become too close to the Yankees, according to West. West goes on to say that his insistence on taking the surname Williams (his name during the dreadful days of slavery had been Lewis Pope) only confirmed her belief that "Uncle Lewis" had become too independent.

The truth is, according to West, after 1865 Rev. Lewis Williams "busied himself helping other freedmen find land, and by the late fall (of 1865) he was involved in a Freedmen's Bureau plan to settle former slaves from Wilkes County" elsewhere. Additionally, he was perceived to have been addressing the rights of newly freed black people in his sermons. This was regarded as politics.

This perception of mixing politics with preaching, disloyalty, and independence is apparently why Rev. Lewis Williams was unable to get his license to preach renewed by First Baptist Church. Rev Williams' had been preaching for well over 25 years but his application for renewal of his license to preach was denied a second time.

At the same time, formerly enslaved African Americans all over the South were anxious to exercise their rights as independent citizens to establish their own churches where they were not limited in the leadership positions they could hold and where they could worship without supervision of others.

In her 2000 book entitled *Appointed to Tell,* Cecelia Gartrell Evans, great-granddaughter of Rev. Williams states that "on July 17, 1868 Freedman Baptist Church (later called Springfield) was organized. Apparently both names were used until 1869. Letters of Organization were granted from the Greenwood Baptist Church in Barnett, Georgia where Rev. Peter Johnson was the pastor.

Among those present with letters from First Baptist Church of Washington for the Organization were: Brother Jesse Chivers and his wife, Brother George O'Neal and his wife, Brother Dennis Cox, Brother Robert Butler and his wife, Brother Henry Hammons and his wife, Sister Harriett Hawkins, Brother Elisha Gilbert, Brother Mansfield Starks, Brother Willis Anderson, and Rev. Lewis Williams and his wife, Rachael. Rev. Williams was ordained by Rev. Johnson and was chosen to serve as pastor. Brother Andrew Lewis was elected to serve as Church Clerk."

Cecelia Gartrell Evans goes on to say that "Thomas Williams, the administrator and executor of Freedman, also called Springfield Baptist Church, purchased more or less one acre of land from Charlie Jones for the sum of twenty-one dollars." The land was conveyed to the Trustee and their successors. Original trustees were Brothers Thomas Williams, Elisha Gilbert, Robert Binns, and Jesse Chivers.

As membership grew under the leadership of Rev. Williams, the church obtained, in 1869, the services of outstanding African American contractor and carpenter, Mr. Edward Bonner to build their first edifice. Pastor Lewis Williams was himself an accomplished carpenter.

Crowds flocked to Springfield to hear Rev. Williams' eloquent preaching and to hear soul stirring singing from the church choir recently organized by Brother William Bowen. A Sunday School was organized with William Bowen serving as Sunday School Superintendent until 1875. He was succeeded in that position by Sophie Williams Scott, daughter of Rev. Williams. She served for 30 years as Sunday School Superintendent.

Washington loved the singing of Springfield's choir. They held many concerts to raise money for the building of a brick edifice and to purchase an organ. Construction of the brick edifice began in 1883.

In her 2001 book entitled *Appointed to Tell More*, Cecelia Gartrell Evans continues to share her research on the life of Rev. Lewis Williams and Springfield Baptist Church. With regard to the role of Springfield as the Mother Church to seven offspring churches, she states that "During these times of growth and development, some members of the church who traveled many miles to attend services decided it was feasible to consider building in their own communities.

These daughter churches that were granted letters of dismissal from Springfield were: Booker's Chapel, 1874; Cherry Grove, 1875; Gibson Grove, 1885; Young's Chapel, 1885; Twin Oak, 1886; Hilliard Station, 1896; and Mt. Carmel, 1901."

Rev. Williams preached the Word of God with power and persuasion until God called him home in 1906 at age 85. Few, if any, ministers in Wilkes County or anywhere, in any era, can assert that the ministry God has given them has led to the establishment of seven offspring churches that have remained viable for more than 100 years.

To God be the glory for the life, ministry, and work of Rev. Lewis Williams. He followed God's instructions, not the will of man in establishing Springfield Baptist Church. The community and entire town of Washington grew to love, respect and follow him, because he followed Christ. He is unquestionably, an Unsung Hero of Wilkes County, Georgia.

Chapter 2

REV. ALBERT T. ZELLARS
1904 - 2004

God-sent preacher and teacher of the Gospel of Christ (February, 2007)

Distinguished African American Baptist minister and educator, Rev. Albert Theodore Roosevelt Zellars was born August 8, 1904, in Lincoln County, Georgia, to George Pierce Zellars, a farmer, and Emma Louise Hawes Zellars, a homemaker. He was educated in the public/church schools of Lincoln County. He then attended Morehouse College in Atlanta, which later became the alma mater of Dr. Martin Luther King, Jr.

A lifelong member of Harmony Baptist Church in Lincoln County, Rev. Zellars returned to Lincoln and Wilkes County after college where he taught in the public schools for many years. However, his primary "calling," which he accepted at age 16, was to be a minister of the gospel of Jesus Christ. While he pastored numerous churches in Lincoln and Wilkes Counties, most noteworthy are his 47 years of service at Mulberry Baptist Church in the Sandtown Community and his 21 years at New Ford Baptist Church in Danburg.

During his first pastorate at New Ford Baptist Church (1935-1943), which partially coincided with the years of his pastorate at nearby Mulberry Baptist Church, New Ford grew and was a meaningful and viable spiritual, social, and educational force in the Danburg community. With the able support and assistance of such outstanding deacons as Charlie Cofer, Willie Cofer, J. C. Brewer, D. J. Bradley, John R. Bradley, Cap Robinson, Gordon Walton and many others, New Ford Church School was expanded and became the only school in northeast Wilkes County to have a junior high school for African American children.

Another outstanding young recent Morehouse graduate, Professor John Henry Jackson, was called to serve as principal of the junior high and elementary school. His wife, Hattie Jackson served as a teacher in the New Ford Elementary School. They are the parents of the current Washington-Wilkes Comprehensive High School principal, Andrew Jackson.

During the concurrent tenures of Zellars and Jackson at New Ford, they influenced the lives of hundreds of students of color who successfully studied at the elementary and junior high school. Graduates of New Ford Junior High School include present and former Wilkes Countians such as Veola Cofer Anderson, Gartrel Robinson, Arthur Danner, Carrie Hudson Mays, Ethel Mae Anderson Johnson, Regina Cofer Burnett, Lee Cofer, Willie T. Cofer, Herbert Chennault, Bertha Jackson Singleton, Jesse Jackson, Mary Lee Dunn, Elizabeth Sims, and many others.

These junior high school graduates gained further education and training elsewhere and made an impact in their community and their world. The children and grandchildren of many of them are college graduates and professionals. Zellars pastored New Ford a second time from 1960 until 1973 and continued his superb Christian example, service, and commitment to doing the will of

God.

Rev. Zellars spent 47 years (1938-1985) as pastor of Mulberry Baptist Church in the Sandtown Community. Among his members in 1978 was Deacon Albert Rucker, chairman of the deacon board. Rucker had been a member since he was a lad of seven or eight years of age. He recalls when he would sometime begin the six- or seven-mile trek from his home to Mulberry for Saturday church conference and Zellars would often come along and give him a ride in his car. Few people of color owned cars in those days, so it was really a treat to be offered a ride by Pastor Zellars.

Rucker recalls what history now records as Zellars' finest hour of Christian leadership at Mulberry. It occurred in 1978 when three young white teenage boys, after an evening of intoxication, set fire to Mulberry Baptist Church and three other historic African American churches. Upon receiving word of the destruction by fire of Mulberry, Zellars simply wept.

After a while, he composed himself and responded to Rucker, who had brought the awful news to him, by simply saying, "The Lord will provide." The community reached out to help. New Ford, a "fourth Sunday" church, immediately made its sanctuary and other church facilities available for Mulberry's "third Sunday" worship services.

The three young men were arrested and confessed to burning the churches. Rucker recalls that after several weeks of prayer and meditation, Zellars said to him that the Lord had revealed to him that he and Mulberry Church should forgive the young men for burning the church. While Rucker says that he declined to respond at the time, it did not take him very long to remember that he and his wife were the parents of several children and if one of them got into trouble, he would want someone to have compassion on them.

Rucker immediately gave his full support to Zellars by presenting the proposal for church forgiveness of the young men to the church body at conference. The Mulberry church family unanimously agreed to forgive.

Zellars went a step farther. He appeared in court and asked the judge to be merciful on the young men. Reports of this magnanimous act of love and forgiveness soon appeared on the local, state, and national news. Rucker's phone began ringing day and night. People from all races, regions, religions and vocations wanted to know what they could do to help rebuild Mulberry. The first contribution of $4,000 arrived from West Virginia. Other generous contributions followed. Rev. Albert Huyck, Jr., and other local religious, business, and political leaders began a "Rebuilding Fellowship Fund" and encouraged people from Wilkes and surrounding counties to contribute financially.

Mulberry hired an architect, Henry Whitehead, who also agreed to serve as foreman for a three day construction "blitz" on March 16-18, 1978. Rucker states that he left home on the morning of March 16, 1978, expecting to put in a long day's work with just a few people. But to his amazement, at the prescribed time more than 150 men from as far away as Missouri converged on the site. Some were carpenters, brick masons, plumbers, and electricians. Many were semi-skilled. All "had a mind to work" and got the job done.

The beautiful edifice they erected during that glorious three day period stands today to the glory of God, the Father. Its construction is a testament to the power of love over hate, the power of forgiveness over unforgiveness, and the power of good over evil.

When God called 99-year-old Rev. Albert T. Zellars home on April 28, 2004, He summoned one of His sincere "servant leaders" who had left for us, the living, a legacy of love, forgiveness, service, commitment, integrity, scholarship, and living peaceably with ones' fellow man.

Of Zellars, Rucker says that "he was my pastor, my teacher, my preacher, my mentor, my counselor, and my friend to the very end. He was a God-sent preacher and teacher of the gospel of Jesus Christ." The Wilkes and Lincoln County community would agree that Rev. Albert T. Zellars was indeed a God-sent man.

The community would agree, as well, that from 1939 until 2004, Zellars could have had no better friend, deacon, or student than Albert Rucker. As long as Rucker or any of his sons live; as long as the present pastor of Mulberry, Rev. Robert Crawford, lives; as long as the many preachers of the gospel and members of Mulberry and New Ford who sat under the teachings of Zellars live, then Zellars lives - for indeed, he touched us all with his love and with the teachings of Jesus.

Chapter 3

BLACK CHURCHES OF WILKES COUNTY

African-American history reflected in Black churches (February, 2008)

Distinguished African American scholars like W.E.B. DuBois, E. Franklin Frazier, and C. Eric Lincoln have regularly pointed out that one cannot study the history of African American people without studying the African American church. Accordingly, we explore in this article one of Wilkes County's oldest and most significant black churches.

In his publication entitled "A History of New Ford Church," Rev. J. H. Fortson suggests in 1882 that the church acquired its name because of its nearness to New Ford Creek. Founded in 1795, New Ford is one of the oldest churches in Wilkes County.

When the original New Ford Baptist church was built in 1795, George Washington was still in office as the first president of the United States. Congress had ratified the United States Constitution a mere six years earlier. Georgia had been admitted to the Union a mere seven years earlier. The first U.S. census ever taken (1790) had revealed that people of color made up 19.3% of the country's population.

Eli Whitney had introduced the cotton gin two years earlier, which would make Wilkes County the "Cotton Capital of the World" and would make cotton growing profitable in many other places throughout the South thus instilling new life into the slave economy.

Native Americans would soon be forced to endure the Trail of Tears and be "ethnically cleansed" from Georgia and other parts of the southeast portion of the country. Descendants of Africa had been in bondage in this country for more than 175 years and would not be free or counted as American citizens until after the Civil War - some 75 years later.

As the sons and daughters of kings and queens, princesses and potentates, warriors and mothers, griots and medicine men, our ancestors, today's African Americans, had been snatched from their native Africa and inhumanely brought through the middle passage and forced into enslavement in this far and distant land. Prohibited from learning to read or write or communicate in their own language, each generation lost more and more of its native culture, language, and knowledge of Mother Africa.

At the same time, these descendants of the builders of the Sphinx and Pyramids of Africa; these offspring of those who taught mathematics and science to the Greeks and the rest of the world; these inventors of the world's first large scale irrigation system were expected to and did build the many gigantic antebellum homes found all over Wilkes County. With their own hands, they built New Ford Baptist Church and many other churches in Wilkes County, even though they could not join them and could only sit on the back pew or in the balcony while white Christians carried on the services. But this didn't stop them from believing in the concept of one omnipotent, omnipresent, and omniscient God who is creator of all of us.

For in Mother Africa, our ancestors had been a deeply spiritual people. They had lived on the same continent inhabited by Abraham after he and his wife, Sarah, came up out of Ur of the Chaldenes; and where Joseph had been first a slave, then a prisoner, and later second in charge in Egypt. Our persecuted ancestors were from the land where Mary and Joseph had taken the baby Jesus to flee from Herod's order to kill all the boy babies under two years old. They were from the land where God told Moses to go and tell old Pharaoh to "let my people go."

New Ford's early attendees of color identified greatly, as do blacks today, with the concept of God delivering oppressed people from the shackles of slavery and oppression and this story would inspire them and us, as no other, in our fight for freedom and justice in this land.

And so, while our fore-parents sat on the back pews or in balconies as they worshipped and began to live Christianity, their descendants would learn and teach the rest of the story - that Mother Africa is the physical setting for a large portion of the Old Testament and some of the New Testament. Their descendants would know that many of the early church fathers, such as St. Augustine, Origen, Tertullian, and many others were actually born in, lived in, and taught the Scriptures in Africa.

In fact, the foremost and official catechism school of the first 200 years of Christianity was located on the continent of Africa. Many studied at the Alexandrian School, in Egypt. Origen studied at the school under Clement and was later head of the school. So you see, God in his infinite wisdom worked through our African ancestors in forging and shaping the Christian faith from the first century to the present.

The July 25, 1936, report of the committee of the history of New Ford Baptist Church states that when New Ford moved to its present location in 1832 (on land donated by William McLendon), people of color were for the first time allowed to unite as members of New Ford.

In his compilation entitled *"Minutes of Danburg Baptist Church, (formerly New Ford Baptist Church) Wilkes County, Georgia,"* Ray B. Stevens presents a summary of the minutes of the New Ford Baptist Church conference on November 30, 1834, and thereafter. These minutes reflect that a special church conference was convened each month for people of color rather than have them participate with the white congregation.

In the September 1857 minutes is found the church statistics. New Ford had 125 members of whom 49 were white and 86 were people of color. Black members were in a majority before the Civil War.

In the July 10, 1858 minutes, the white congregation in their church conference discussed moving to a new church, as did they again in the August 1858 and September 1858 conference.

In the November 11, 1866 minutes, a specific request was made that the colored members of the congregation be allowed to have separate worship services at New Ford.

In the January 7, 1871 minutes, the white congregation in church conference voted to "adopt a motion to let the colored members of the church have the use of the house..."

And so, the minutes make it clear that the transition from the original congregation to the present congregation did not occur in a single month or even a single year. The transition evolved over a period of time. All things considered, the present congregation, for more than a century, has been comfortable with 1870 as the time frame in which the present era of the church began.

The argument could very well be made that it was earlier. In fact, it could be asserted in 1795, believers erected New Ford to the glory and honor of God the Father and it matters not whether God's people are black or white. We all are children of the most High God.

Nevertheless, a new social order had begun to evolve inside the church prior to the Civil War and the personalities and demographics would strongly favor people of color. And so, a building use and occupancy policy based on the demographics and leadership of the Holy Spirit was reasonable.

The August 9, 1878 minutes reflect that the "committee made arrangements to sell this house and build a new one in Danburg. Report that they made the following arrangement with white Danburg merchant, Mr. John L. Anderson, that he agreed to take this house and build us a new one in Danburg as good or better than this one, free of costs, to us and the committee reserves the burying grounds here."

In 1879, the people of color of New Ford began their purchase of the church and approximately six acres of land on which it stands from the John L. Anderson family. They continued to call their church New Ford. The first Board of Trustees of the new New Ford consisted of Bro. Moses Standard; Bro. Anderson Sutton; Bro. Edmund Tate, Sr.; Bro. Raff Jones; and Bro. Peter Walton. An additional 1 ½ acres was purchased in 1913.

Clearly, occupancy, use, and leadership of the present congregation by people of color occurred many years before transfer of title to the church building.

The present congregation of New Ford stands alone in northeast Wilkes County as a church where the descendants of loyal, faithful, and dedicated church members rose to leadership within the walls of the church of their enslaved ancestors through their love for the church, love for their brethren, and the love of God through Jesus. Their foreparents once worshipped from the back pews, but they seized the time and circumstances and rose up and purchased the church and they have maintained it for the ensuing decades to the glory and honor of God the Father.

God has brought them a mighty long way. In an article which appeared in the Washington *News-Reporter* commemorating the bicentennial of New Ford/Danburg Baptist (dated October 5, 1995), Mrs. Mildred Sisson states that "The usual separation saw blacks building churches. Most whites can name a black church started by former members of their church." In the case of New Ford, it is the mother church.

Pastor James White Jr. has served as pastor since 2000. Under his leadership, New Ford Baptist Church is growing spiritually, numerically, and physically. As New Ford proceeds into the 21st century, many new members and ministries are coming into being.

New Ford welcomes you to visit and when you get tired of visiting, you are welcomed to join.

Chapter 4

WILKES COUNTY SUNDAY SCHOOL UNION

Bible Bowl teams evolve from dedicated SSU participants (February, 2010)

It is imperative that every community, county, state and nation have deeply rooted institutions to remind its members of the values, traditions, precepts, and culture of that entity from generation to generation. The Black Church and more specifically, for purposes of this article, The Wilkes County Sunday School Union has been a strong and viable institution in the religious, cultural, social, and civic development of the young people of Wilkes County for more than one hundred and twenty years.

The Lincoln, Elbert, Wilkes County Sunday School Union was set in motion on May 5, 1889 when Brother G. B. Blakey of New Ford Baptist Church brought a resolution to the New Ford Sunday School proposing the organization of the Sunday School Union. With the concurrence of the pastor, Rev. Calvin Lockhart, New Ford decided to accept the challenge so long as there was no conflict with regular Sunday worship services. Pastor C. H. Holloway of Gibson Grove Baptist volunteered to "open the doors of Gibson Grove for the Union to come in and organize."

On June 18, 1889, four buggy loads of dedicated Sunday school attendees traveled to Gibson Grove and established the Union. Founders are G. B. Blakey of New Ford Sunday School, G. W. Walton, Superintendent of New Ford Sunday School, Rev. C. H. Holloway, pastor of Gibson Grove, Rev. R. V. Sutton and Brother J. C. Sutton of Mt. Carmel, S. C. The Union elected A. M. Holloway of Lincoln County as its first president and Amanda Dallas of Lincoln County as its first Secretary.

Over the years there have been as many as forty Sunday Schools enrolled. Union presidents over the years have included Deacon Sam Anderson of Mulberry Baptist Church, Deacon Albert Rucker, Sr. and Rev. Albert Rucker, Jr. of Mulberry Baptist Church. Deacon Statham McLendon of Trinity Baptist Church, Deacon Cary Ware of Pompeys Chapel, Deacon Edward Drinkard of Pompeys Chapel, Deacon (now Rev.) Tommy Johnson of Pleasant Grove, Deacon Eddie Bankston of Pleasant Grove, Deacon Larry Smith of Trinity, Deacon Jamie Johnson of Pleasant Grove, Deacon Charles Morgan of Springfield and many others.

Secretaries/assistant secretaries over the years have included Ella Ware of Springfield, Verna Bradley of Trinity, Doris Irvin of Mt. Carmel, Robin Booker of Mt. Carmel, and Melvene Binns of Mulberry. Present secretaries, Robin Booker and Melvene Binns have served more than 20 years each as secretary and assistant secretary respectively, of the Sunday School Union and they have been quite active in the development of students in their Sunday Schools and in the community. Deacon Willie Moses Jenkins of Hilliard Station Baptist Church served as Treasurer for more than 24 years until his recent passing.

Literally hundreds of Wilkes County young people made their first public speech at a Sunday School Union event. Hundreds more were elected to serve in their first elective office as a youth or adult. Sill more were helped through college or trade school with scholarship assistance from the Union. Most present day Wilkes County Sunday School Superintendents, teachers, and other church workers got their start in their Sunday Schools and in the Union. Many young people first met the person who was later to become their spouse during quarterly Sunday School Union Activities.

In recent years, a new category of dedicated Sunday School Union participants has evolved. They are the coaches of the Bible Bowl teams. They are involved Sunday School Superintendents and teachers and parents who spend a great deal of time throughout the year teaching, re-teaching, drilling and coaching our young people on the contents of the weekly Sunday School lessons as they prepare to demonstrate their knowledge of the Word of God during Bible Bowl competition.

Among these outstanding Bible Bowl coaches are John Jackson of Springfield, Francine Towns and Deacon Johnny Bankston of Pleasant Grove, Robin Booker of Mt Carmel, and many others. Much appreciation also goes to Rachael Jackson of Gibson Grove for her impeccable scorekeeping, Kathryn Anderson of New Ford for her precise operation of our electronic buzzer system, and to all the adults who work so hard to have a meaningful Bible Bowl each quarter.

While the above listed adult Christian leaders are "unsung heroes" for their work in the vineyard over the last 120 years, our young students who are preparing themselves by participation in the Bible Bowl and other Union activities are "unsung heroes," as well. They will be tomorrow's Sunday School superintendents, teachers, church officers, preachers of the gospel, and leaders in the community. They are all unsung heroes.

Chapter 5

REV. KENNETH WALKER

Pastor, local, national and international leader (February, 2009)

Distinguished African American pastor, civic and government leader, Rev. Kenneth Walker was born in Wilkes County in 1966 and was raised by his grandmother, the late Mrs. Bessie Mae Hayes. An extremely gifted student, he initially dreamed of becoming an astronaut or medical doctor. At the age of 18, he felt the call of God on his life to become a minister of the Gospel of Jesus Christ.

He was licensed and ordained and spent the following seven years earning his undergraduate degree at Paine College and his Master's of Divinity Degree at The Interdenominational Theological Center's Morehouse School of Religion prayerfully developing his leadership and academic skills. He was elected Student Government President at both schools and was called to his first pastorate at 22 years of age, while still a seminary student.

Initially, as a bi-vocational pastor, Rev. Walker spent thirteen years serving in several key positions in the Georgia State Capitol.

During this political "season" of his life, God granted him unprecedented favor with both black and white elected and appointed officials. Rev. Walker served as the first African-American Executive Assistant to a Georgia Lieutenant Governor; the first Chief of Staff for Georgia's first and the South's only African-American State Senate Majority Leader; and the first African-American Executive Assistant appointed to the Georgia Regional Transportation Authority.

Rev. Walker energetically worked in the re-election Campaign of President Bill Clinton in 1996 and went on to serve on the President's Ministerial Roundtable in 2000. He helped to pass the HOPE Scholarship. He is proud to have had a major role in passing legislation that overhauled the state's Medicaid, healthcare and social services systems. Additionally, he worked on legislation that mandated insurance companies to cover mammograms for women. Moreover, he worked on the legislation that required insurance companies to permit women to stay in the hospital for an extra day after giving birth to a child.

A strong advocate for development of our youth, Rev. Walker co-founded the Personal Development Program for Juvenile Delinquents in the State of Georgia. He led weekly motivational and self-value seminars for students who were committed to the State. Additionally, he founded the Church Juvenile Program Pavilion of Hope which is a Church based preventive and rehabilitative program which utilizes the services of mentors to provide a network of support in the lives of young men and women by using a holistic approach. The program is still being used in several Georgia counties.

In the summer of 2001, Rev. Walker was called to serve as Pastor of Shoal Creek Baptist Church in Locust Grove, Georgia. Shoal has a long and storied history, having been pastured by Dr. Martin Luther King, Sr. in the 1930s. During Rev. Walker's three year tenure as Pastor, the church experienced tremendous growth in membership, Sunday School attendance, Bible study attendance, and contributions in tithes and offerings.

Moreover, “Da Creek” as it is affectionately called, gave birth to a Praise Team, Dance Team, Step Ministry, Two Friday Night Live with Jesus Services, Leadership Training for all officers including the Deacons and Trustees Ministry, Men’s and Women’s Bible Study, development of a Christian Education Department, New Members orientation, Judah Fest, Sunday School Teacher Training, and a “Stages of Black History” (play written by Rev. Walker). The church organized a Men’s and Women’s Ministry, as well. The first woman was licensed to preach in the church’s history. The church launched its local cable television broadcast in April 2003.

In August 2004, Rev. Walker was led to organize in Locust Grove, Georgia, the Gospel Tabernacle Praise and Worship Center which became The Tabernacle of Praisc Christian Church in 2005. God has blessed them with explosive growth in membership and attendance on Sunday mornings and Wednesday nights. In June of 2007, Rev. Walker was inspired to establish the Bessie Mae Hayes Memorial Scholarship in honor of his grandmother who raised him. Scholarships are awarded to students at the Church who excel in academics, community life and in their Church life.

God has sent new spiritual mentors into Rev. Walker’s life during the last eight years. Bishop Noel Jones, Dr. Joe Ratliff, and Dr. Sherry Gaither have been instrumental in his continued spiritual growth. In 2004, he was invited to accompany Bishop Noel Jones to South Africa where they preached at two annual conferences together. Since that time, God has opened a new door of ministry for Rev. Walker in South Africa.

Extremely active in his community, Rev. Walker has been a proud member of Alpha Phi Alpha Fraternity, Inc. since 1986. Presently, he is in his second term as President of the Nu Mu Lambda Chapter in Decatur, Georgia. In 2007, his Chapter honored him with the prestigious Augustus M. Witherspoon Leadership Award for outstanding leadership in his fraternity, community, and chosen profession. On April 20, 2008, Rev. Walker was sworn in as the Chartering President of the National Pan-Hellenic Council, Inc. of DeKalb County, Georgia. In that capacity he leads the "Divine Nine" Black Greek Fraternities and Sororities.

Some of Rev. Walker's awards include Who's Who Among American College and University Students, Rev. Jesse Jackson Leadership Award, Outstanding Young Men in America Award, Martin Luther King, Jr. Oratorical Award, Reese J. Booker Scholarship Award, and College Student of the Year during his senior year at Paine College.

Rev. Walker is the father of Terrence and Sydney.

Of Rev. Kenneth Walker, Deacon Albert Rucker of Mulberry Baptist Church states "I came to know Rev. Walker as he grew into his teenage years. I was present when he accepted Jesus Christ into his life. What drew me to Rev. Walker was his testimony about Jesus Christ as a young boy. Kenneth was led by a God-fearing Grandmother, who instilled that same fear into Kenneth. He was eager to know the truth about God's word. He was very sensitive and dedicated. Most of all, he was very likeable. God had given him a vision at a very young age, and I believe he is being true to that vision."

Former Washington-Wilkes high school teacher and administrator, Mr. Eddie Finnell, states "Kenneth Walker was president of his high school class (1984). He was an intelligent, respectable student with great leadership ability. He was a garrulous, sociable, approachable person, always greeting people with a smile. His goal was to be a productive citizen and to never forget his roots. These traits are still prevalent as shown through his magnanimous contributions to society."

"As a young boy Kenneth Walker worked hard to be the best. During Sunday School he was always ready and eager to answer questions and joined in on the discussions or rather lead the discussions. His leadership skills were very impressive for such a young student. Kenneth was always prepared for class and displayed wisdom in his actions, so I was not surprised when I learned he had been called into ministry. Given the opportunity, I knew he would excel" says Mrs. Minnie Evans, one of his former Sunday School teachers.

Rev. Kenneth Walker's lifetime of learning, teaching, preaching, and leading at the local, state, national, and international level in both the religious and civic arena, propels him into being a highly regarded Unsung Hero of Wilkes County, Georgia.

Chapter 6

DEACON ALBERT RUCKER, SR.

Making a positive impact on the lives of fellow citizens (February, 2010)

When the oldest son of Deacon Albert Rucker, Sr., Deacon Joe Lewis Rucker made his transition from labor to reward on October 18, 2009, he left to mourn his wife, Alfreeda, sons Shawn and Martin and two grandchildren.

Additionally, he left to cherish his memories, his brothers, Rev. Albert, Jr. and Johnny and sisters Annie Kate Cullars and Mamie Mills, and a host of nieces, nephews, other family members, coworkers, and fellow citizens. Moreover, he left his caring stepmother, Mrs. Elmira Rucker and his loving father, Deacon Albert Rucker, Sr.

As the oldest of five children in the Rucker family, he had been the ideal older son and older brother. His natural mother, the late Annie Lee Rucker died after he and his siblings had reached adulthood, but he was blessed to continue to feel a mothers' love from his stepmother.

A serious minded young man, Joe graduated from Washington Central High School in 1965 and chose to serve his country by entering the Marine Corps where he received two Purple Hearts for very serious injuries received during two separate tours of combat duty in Viet Nam. Upon being honorably discharged he continued his personal and professional development which led to marriage and family and ultimately, a career with the US Postal Service that lasted 27 years.

He followed in his father's footsteps and was a faithful member of their ancestral family church, Mulberry Baptist Church in the Sandtown Community and was Chairman of the Deacon Board. Joe had served in the highest position in Shiloh Masonic Lodge #63, that of Worshipful Master. He owned a farm and cattle and had a passion for the outdoors. His obituary states that he never met a stranger and he was always willing to help those in need. He loved his family and he regularly took time to visit his father and stepmother at lunch time or to stop by in the afternoon after a long days work at the post office and sit on his father's front porch to fellowship with his brothers and his dad. Deacon Albert, Sr. counted his son Joe among his best friends in life.

Deacon Rucker states that he thanks God for each of his children and he loves and cherishes each one of them. Joe was unique in that he was his first born and he accepted his home training well. He grew up to be a good, descent, and honorable man who set the right kind of example for his younger siblings, his children, his church, and the rest of our community. He states that he thanks God for placing Joe in our midst for sixty two wonderful years. He is grateful for the Christian life he lived and the example and legacy he leaves behind.

Deacon Rucker strongly believes that parents ought to do everything they can to maintain their families. He states that families are the key and foundation to a strong community and nation. He believes that parents must keep Christ at the center of their family and they must be committed to making their marriage work. They must learn to work things out, for so many are hurt when families are separated, he says. He further states that parents must continue to work harder at training their children in the way they should go. They should regularly take their children to Sunday School and church. Deacon Rucker recalls a time when he was the driver of a 60 passenger church bus that picked up and brought children to Mulberry each Sunday for Sunday School.

During that time, he had twelve grandchildren in Sunday School and singing in the church choir, and one of his grandchildren, Cheryl, played the piano for the choir. He states that children should be taught to tell the truth and never tell a lie. They should be taught to never take anything that does not belong to them. They should be taught to respect themselves, their elders, and others. Deacon Rucker cites the Book of Proverbs to make his next point; "A good name is rather to be chosen than great riches." He asserts that we ought to teach our children to live upright lives so as never to discredit their name or their families' names.

He goes on to say that "parents should require their children to be good students and stay in school until they at least graduate from high school. He states that student dropouts are hurting our families, our communities, and our country. The youngsters who drop out are limiting their futures. He adds that no one knows that better than himself. Having grown up during the era of sharecropping and restricted opportunity for schooling for blacks, he has emphasized to his children and grandchildren the importance of education. His oldest grandchild, Cheryl Rucker Whittiker, now a medical doctor, has led the way to higher academic achievement for his eighteen grandchildren and five great grandchildren.

Since Deacon Rucker moved into the city from the Sandtown Community in 1951, he has witnessed many changes in the physical and political landscape of Washington. Urban renewal, during the leadership of Mayor Ed Pope enabled the paving of roads and the cleaning up of many areas. Involvement of black citizens in city government has greatly increased. Deacon Rucker recalls a phone call he made to Mayor Pope in the mid 60s suggesting that the city do more to better prepare for integration. Deacon Rucker suggested that a bi-racial council start meeting to create greater understanding between blacks and whites in order to avoid some of the challenges being experienced by some surrounding counties.

Mayor Pope agreed and upon seeking Deacon Rucker's recommendations on the size and content of the bi-racial committee, he went forth with conducting the meetings on a monthly basis. Deacon Rucker says that progress was immediately evident when a white state trooper with a reputation for being insensitive to racial issues expressed his gratitude for the chance to meet and discuss issues.

Additionally, when it was pointed out in one of the sessions that there were no cashiers working in any of the downtown stores, Deacon Rucker states that a progressive downtown merchant and member of the bi-racial council, "Steve Blackman rose to the occasion and hired the first black cashier in Washington, Mrs. Minnie Turman." Other downtown merchants soon followed his example with the employment of blacks in their stores and thereby averted a great deal of racial tension. Steve Blackmon adds that Mrs. Turman remained with his store for the following seventeen years.

Further, he states that "Albert Rucker is a fine person, who uses good common sense to come up with sensible solutions to problems." Rightfully so, Steve Blackmon is proud of the role he, Deacon Rucker, and many others played in ushering Washington through a tough period of social change. As time passed, black police officers were hired, and dialogue continued for some years. Deacon Rucker and others regularly attended City Council meetings to have their issues addressed.

When asked how he and others went about preparing their sons, daughters and others for the oncoming era of integration, he states that they urged them to remember their home training and to be law abiding citizens. The young people were anxious to do their part to bring about change. Deacon Rucker recalls that his daughter, Annie Kate and his son Albert, Jr. were part of a protest march in the mid-1960s to bring about the integration of Washington's all white high school in accordance with the ruling of the 1954 United States Supreme Court case <u>Brown v. Board of Education</u> declaring segregation in public schools to be unconstitutional. Annie Kate, Albert, Jr. and the other young people were arrested, loaded into buses and taken to jail.

Rev. Albert Rucker, Jr. recalls that he and his sister were not released until about 10:30 that night. They were never charged with any offense for they were seeking local compliance with a US Supreme Court decision. Deacon Rucker states that even though the young people were standing up for right, he received a backlash when he reported for work on Monday morning. When his supervisor challenged him to "whip" Annie Kate and Albert, Jr., he declined to do so.

Annie Kate went on to later be elected to the local Board of Education. Albert, Jr. would go on to complete a career in the US Air Force and subsequently be elected to the Washington City Council. Rev. Albert, Jr. states that it was not until years later that his father told him of the backlash at his worksite. He states that he has always respected his father's belief in fairness, equity, and justice, but his respect and admiration for his father became even greater when he found that his dad risked losing his job in standing up for him and Annie Kate.

Although he is now eighty years old and retired from the workforce, Deacon Rucker continues to be actively involved in the lives of his children, grandchildren, great grandchildren, Mulberry Baptist Church, his community and city government. He is blessed to have a loving and supportive wife, Elmira.

When Deacon Rucker and Mrs. Elmira McCord were married, he had five grown children and she had eight grown children – Eleanor, Henry, Clarence, Fannie, Marilyn, Jimmy, Mable, and Dr. Marion (Ph.D.). All of them were and still are high achievers and are doing well in their lives. They are hard-working, God-fearing, good and decent family oriented people who have prospered in their careers and in life. Deacon Rucker has a great deal of love and admiration for them, their spouses, and the eighteen grandchildren and six great-grandchildren they have produced. Together, Deacon and Mrs. Rucker now have 29 loving grandchildren and 10 wonderful great grandchildren.

Deacon Rucker continues to be a strong follower of the teachings of Jesus as initially shared with him by his lifetime friend, mentor, and pastor, Rev. Albert T. Zellars. Through his faith in God and his teaching of the Scriptures, Rev. Zellars helped mold Deacon Rucker into a strong, loving, caring and forgiving Christian servant-leader.

Rev. Albert Huyck, well loved and respected former pastor of First Baptist Church in Washington, Georgia states that "Albert Rucker, Sr. is one of the finest Christians I have ever known, and I have been around a long time and I have known a lot of people." Rev. Huyck recalls that during his work with the Rebuilding Fellowship Fund which had the goal of rebuilding Mulberry Baptist Church after it was destroyed by fire by some unthinking teenagers, the work was a lot easier because of Deacon Rucker's "good common sense and ability to make good quick decisions."

Deacon Rucker wants the nation and especially the City of Washington to continue to grow in love, peace, and in becoming all it is capable of becoming. He wants to help bring about good government for all the people. During Willie Burns' tenure as Mayor of Washington, Georgia he called for five good men of faith to join him and his son, Rev. Albert Rucker, Jr. in sending up daily prayers for our city government, especially for Mayor Willie Burns. Deacon Rucker continues to make a great and positive impact on the lives of his family, friends, fellow Christians, and fellow citizens. Indeed, he is an "Unsung Hero of Wilkes County, Georgia."

Chapter 7

REV. & MRS. HENRY M. EASLEY AND DEACON & MRS. D. W. DUNN

Blessed to have these caring Christian couples in our midst (February, 2010)

It has been my good fortune over the last few years to attend the reaffirmation of wedding vows by two of Wilkes County's finest couples who were each celebrating more than 50 years of happy and successful marriage.

Rev. Henry M. and Mrs. Jacquelyn Moss Easley were married on August 31, 1957 in Washington, Georgia. They renewed their wedding vows on August 30, 2008 after fifty one years of happy and successful marriage. The renewal ceremony was performed by Rev. Gold Walton, Jr. and was attended by scores of guests. They made the decision to reaffirm their marital vows because their children wanted them to have the dream wedding they were not able to have when they started out. Their nearly fifty three years of marriage has been blessed by God with eight wonderful and productive children: Henry, Jr. (wife Wisteria), James (Mary), Sherry (Frank Charles), Carol (Darrell),

Beverly (David Allen), David, John, and Kelvin (Contessa).

Each of their four older children has completed careers in the Armed Forces of the United States and they are retired senior non-commissioned officers working in their second careers. Additionally, their 6th child, David, is in the Air Force Reserves and is working in his civilian career, as well. Their seventh child, John, completed twelve years of active duty and decided to go to work as a government contractor and is presently serving in Kuwait.

Together, they have more than 100 years of honorable military service and have served in some of the more remote and challenging assignments and places in the world. The remaining two children are hardworking dedicated workers in the middle of their careers. God has blessed the Easleys with eighteen beautiful and smart grandchildren and three wonderful great grandchildren. Rev. & Mrs. Easley state that they are so proud of and thankful for all their children, grandchildren, and great grandchildren. They look forward to each new opportunity to see, talk to, and interact with each of them.

The Easleys maintain that they took their marriage vows seriously and they continue to do all they can to live up to their sacred vows to each other and to God. They credit prayer and keeping Christ at the center of their lives as important reasons why they have been able to endure the ups and downs of marriage for so many years. They state that you cannot be a fault finder if you want to be married for a lifetime.

Throughout the years, Mrs. Easley has made the Easley house a home for her husband and children. She has taken seriously the Scriptural verse, "Train up a child in the way he should go, and when he is old, he will not depart from it." With eight children, Rev. Easley is grateful that God gave his wife a spirit to be a stay-at-home mom and devote her time to taking care of the family.

When asked their advice on raising strong and successful children, Mrs. Easley states that "children must be taught to respect themselves and others and to be nice to other people. Children must be taught to tell the truth and to do what is right in God's sight." She goes on to say that "parents must have a firm hand and must not spare the rod. They must bring their children up in the fear and admonition of the Lord, so taking them to Sunday School and church is most important."

A U.S. Army veteran, Rev. Easley accepted the call into the ministry a year before he and Mrs. Easley were married. Throughout all the days of their children's lives, he states that" it has been very important to him to teach their children the difference between right and wrong, and to train up the children in the way they should go." He has always been aware that their children, especially his five sons were watching him and Mrs. Easley, so he felt it very important for them to see him treating Mrs. Easley with love and kindness.

Mrs. Easley has worked to model virtues of a Christian woman for her daughters and sons and to demonstrate love and respect for her husband. It has been important for Rev. Easley that his children see him trying to live the life he is preaching and teaching about. He felt it necessary that he demonstrate the importance of working hard on his regular job, in the family garden, around their home, and in everything he attempted in order to teach his children a good work ethic. It was important that they learn early that if you want to have something, you have to work for it. Each of their children was required to do chores, inside and outside their home, by him and Mrs. Easley as they were growing up. They are not afraid of work hard. This has contributed greatly to their success in life.

Rev. and Mrs. Easley have been active in the Baptist Church all of their lives. Shady Grove is the home church of Rev. Easley and he is the pastor of St. John and Trinity Baptist Churches. Trinity is the home church of Mrs. Easley where she serves as First Lady, Member of the Mothers Board, and Special Occasion (birthday and anniversary) Announcer.

What a blessing Rev. and Mrs. Easley have been to each other, to their children, their grandchildren, and to the Wilkes County Community as a loving, caring, Christian couple and parents of wonderful and successful children and grandchildren. Indeed, they are "Unsung Heroes of Wilkes County." We are blessed and so grateful to have them in our midst.

Deacon D. W. Dunn and Mrs. Mary Lee Smith Dunn were married on March 27, 1954 in Washington, Georgia. In a wedding ceremony, performed by Rev. Robert Walton in the presence of a full wedding party and scores of guests, they reaffirmed their vows on April 3, 2004 after more than 50 years of happy marriage. They made the decision to reaffirm their vows because of their gratitude to God for allowing them to reach that milestone. Additionally, they were not able to have a wedding when they first got married, so they decided that this was a wonderful opportunity to do so and to affirm their commitment to each other.

During their now nearly 56 years of marriage, God has blessed them with five wonderful and productive children, Dorothy Ann (Roy L.)Gresham of Springfield, VA., Daniel, Jr. of Rome, GA., Lee Allen Dunn of Charlotte, N.C., Danny (Jeanette) of Washington, GA., and Larry (Vestine) of Washington, GA. The Dunns have been blessed with twelve beautiful and smart grandchildren and three darling great grandchildren.

When asked to give advice on how to make one's marriage last a lifetime, they respond that they took an oath before God and man "til death do us part." They meant it when they repeated their vows to one another and they mean it now. In other words, there are no exit signs in their marital relationship. Mrs. Dunn further states that "couples must have God in their lives in order to endure the ups and downs that will come their way."

Moreover, she states that "couples must never stop communicating. They must love one another and be faithful to one another. They must learn to build cooperation and understanding between one another." Deacon Dunn adds that "both spouses should be of the same faith and that the husband should take the lead in spiritually guiding his family to follow the teachings of Jesus Christ and in keeping his family in church and Sunday School." He points out that "a marriage will be blessed if it consists of not two, but three people; the husband, the wife, and Jesus Christ." Deacon Dunn adds that "a husband must be serious about his responsibilities and about the future of his family."

The Dunns count as their most precious memories the birth of each of their five children and the opportunity to participate in their growth and development into independent, God-fearing adults. While Mrs. Dunn is semi-retired from a career that spans 45 years at Wills Memorial Hospital as a Nursing Assistant, Deacon Dunn actively continues his career as a truck driver which he began when he returned to Wilkes County after completing five years of dedicated and honorable service in the United States Army back in the 1950's.

He speaks proudly of the opportunities and relationships he has had over the years at his various places of employment. Clearly, from the onset, the Dunns have felt it important to model a good work ethic for their children and now for their grandchildren. Moreover, three of the Dunn children chose to serve in the military; Dorothy, Danny, and Larry. Larry completed a 20 year career in the United States Marine Corps and since his recent retirement, he continues to proudly serve in his second career as a JROTC instructor at Thomson High School.

During Deacon Dunn's five years of active duty in the Army, Mrs. Dunn and their first two children were able to accompany him during their two year assignment to Fort Leonard Wood, Missouri (Daniel, Jr. was born while they were stationed there); their 17 month assignment to Kaiserslaten, West Germany; and on his final assignment to Fort McCoy, Wisconsin. She vividly remembers the challenges of her thirteen day trip, by ship, with their oldest daughter and oldest son to join her husband in Germany.

A beautiful, caring and loving Christian couple, the Dunns are quite active in the church. They have maintained membership in their ancestral churches since worship services, until recently, have occurred on different Sundays of the month. A lifelong member of Youngs Chapel, Deacon Dunn is Chairman of the Deacon Board and Superintendent of the Sunday School.

A lifelong member of New Ford Baptist Church, Sister Dunn is President of the Mothers' Ministry, Church Treasurer, Trustee, and she serves on the Choir and Kitchen committee. They are quite active in both churches and are very supportive of each other.

With regard to raising children, Deacon and Mrs. Dunn offer the following advice to young parents: "Raise your children in the church. Take them to Sunday School and other activities of the church. Pray fervently for them each day.

Be mindful of who their friends are. Don't allow them to get mixed up with the wrong crowd. Communicate with them throughout the day each day. Maintain a firm hand. Discipline them and make sure they know that you love them and that you have high expectations of them. Train up your children in the way they should go. Trust God. Lean and depend on Him."

Deacon and Mrs. Dunn are a loving, caring, Christian couple who make a positive difference in the lives of their children, grandchildren, and the community at large. Indeed they are "Unsung Heroes of Wilkes County." We are so grateful and so blessed to have them in our midst.

Chapter 8

REV. ROY L. BURNS, SR.
1933 - 2009

"He came through many dangers, toils, and snares" (February, 2011)

Distinguished African American Special Forces soldier, community leader, and Baptist minister, Roy L. Burns, Sr. was born on Christmas day 1933 in Washington, GA and was the third of six children born to Robert Burns, a saw mill worker and Annie Bell Tolbert Burns, a homemaker. His paternal grandparents, Ed and Cassie Slayton Burns were born shortly after the end of the Civil War as were his maternal grandparents John and Lizza Thomson Tolbert.

A 1953 graduate of Washington High School, he and Addie Danner Burns had been married for 56 years at the time of his death in 2009. To that union was born seven children (Roy, Jr., Willie, Nedra, David, Daniel, Anita, and Lynn). They raised three other children, as well -Darryl, Margo and Yvonne.

Rev. Burns began what was to be an illustrious 21 year career in the U. S. Army in 1954, serving first as an enlisted man in the Corps of Engineers, then as an Intelligence Officer in The Special Forces. The travel and assignment demands of his military career in the Special Forces or Green Berets made it more feasible for his family to remain in Washington where their support system included his family and hers. The entire family was able to accompany him during a three year assignment to Fort Bragg.

The Special Forces are an elite commando unit consisting of the most highly skilled, highly trained soldiers in the U. S. Army. Members possess superb combat skills, are experts in survival skills, and speak other languages. Chief Warrant Officer (CW2) Roy L. Burns was fluent in French and Vietnamese. They hold at least a secret security clearance and go places and do a lot of "heavy lifting" and things for our country that cannot be discussed.

He served in Lebanon, Korea, France, and Germany. Additionally, he served two known tours of duty in and around Viet Nam. It can now be told that during a secret Special Forces mission behind enemy lines into North Viet Nam, he was the sole survivor of a helicopter crash and was missing in action (MIA) for six months. He used the survival skills he had been taught to escape and evade the enemy forces and made his way back to friendly territory.

His wife, Addie states that her husband came home to Washington to be with their family as often as possible, but she prayed daily for him and she understood and supported him in his commitment to his military career. She credits the power of prayer and their extended family network for sustaining her and her family. Together, her husband and children and their spouses have more than 135 years of dedicated active military service to our country.

Moreover, they have many, many years of putting their lives on the line for our country while serving in combat. Four siblings and two of their spouses are now retired from the military and are energetically pursuing second careers.

(L-R) Retired CW2 Roy L. Burns Sr., First Lt Roy L. Burns III and Retired CSM Roy L. Burns Jr.

Three of the grandchildren are serving or have served on active duty. As much as any family in the United States, they have paid their dues. Mrs. Burns states "Roy was patriotic, kind, humble and a committed Christian man. He loved his family, his country and he loved the city of Washington. All of our children loved and respected him and they are 'chips off the old block' – as he would call them. We miss him a lot."

With thirty years of active military service, oldest son, retired Army Command Sergeant Major, Roy Burns, Jr. states that his father was his mentor and role model. "Dad prepared us to be leaders and Army officers. He had progressed through the enlisted ranks and achieved the rank of Sergeant First Class, then earned the rank of Warrant Officer. Dad was a little disappointed when I informed him that I felt that I could better serve as an enlisted man.

My goal was to follow in his footsteps as a non-commissioned officer. I liked the way he led people. I marveled at the powerful positive impact he had on soldiers and people in general when he walked into a room. I set my sights on being the same type of leader and earning the highest enlisted rank and position in the Army. My career went well. Dad was present at my Sergeant Major promotion ceremony, and he and mom pinned on me my Sergeant Major rank.

Later, dad was quite proud when I became the youngest Command Sergeant Major in the entire Army selected to serve at the military Post level. Ultimately, I was Command Sergeant Major of the Corps of Engineers before retirement. My wife, Angela, retired from the Army with 22 years of service. My son, First Lieutenant Roy L. Burns, III is an Army officer with combat tours of duty in Iraq and Afghanistan. My daughter Sasha, served four years in the Air Force. Dad set the example and led the way for us all."

Second son, Honorable Willie Burns, Mayor of the City of Washington states that it has been a blessing to have lived near his parents during most of his adult life. After a two year stint in the military, he began his career in law enforcement that culminated in his assignment as Commander of Post 17, Georgia State Patrol, located in Washington. He appreciates the memories of his dad as a tough taskmaster when he was growing up, but he absolutely cherishes his memories of him as a friend, counselor and confidant during the last few years.

"My father's understanding of the application of leadership principles, coupled with his love and respect for all human beings, and his applications of the teachings of Scripture were a daily inspiration to me. I greatly miss his wisdom, knowledge, counsel, and his unconditional love for me and our entire family. I am thankful for his persistent encouragement, superb example, his dedicated life's work, and his inspiring legacy."

City Administrator, Mike Eskew, states that "it was because of the hard and persistent work of my friend, Roy Burns that the senior citizens of our city and county have a wonderful Center to regularly visit and to call their own. He was an outstanding Executive Director of the Center and he genuinely loved and cared for all the seniors. Roy made a great and positive difference in his family, our community, our county and in our country. We miss him."

REV. ROY L. BURNS, SR. (Part 2)

"He served God, family, community, and country" (February, 2011)

The first federal census to record the presence of any member of the Burns family living in Wilkes County is the 1820 census. It reflects that there were five white Burns family members in the household of Samuel S. Burns and there were five blacks. Through their forced free labor, the black Burns members of the household and their descendents created wealth for the white Burns family until after the end of the Civil War. But the ancestors of Rev. Roy Burns evaluated the situation and concluded, in the words of once enslaved Joseph, of the Old Testament, "what man meant for evil, God meant for good." At the earliest possible opportunity, they decided to purchase property and in essence followed the advice of Booker T. Washington and others to "cast down your buckets where you are."

His apparent deep roots in Wilkes County and in our country account for Rev. Burns' deep love and commitment to the county and country. He and his wife transferred the time honored value of love of country to their children and children's children.

By the time their third child, Nedra was born, the Civil Rights Movement was under way and new opportunities were becoming available to all. David was born next, followed by Daniel. Rev. and Mrs. Burns were present when David graduated from the University of Georgia and was commissioned a Second Lieutenant in the U.S. Army.

Now a retired Major, he is in the midst of a meaningful second career in corporate America. Armed with an undergraduate degree from UGA and now an MBA degree, Daniel, after being commissioned a Second Lieutenant through ROTC completed four years of active service and is now a District Manager for a large transportation company in Texas.

His wife, Joyce is a retired Army nurse with twenty six years of service. Daniel vividly recalls his dad's commitment to fairness, honesty, and doing the right thing. He remembers that his father was a man of much humility and of few words. Rather, he was a man of action. He asserts that his dad did not believe in luck. He believed that education and hard work are the keys to success in life.

Daughter, Anita chose a career in the Army, as well. Now retired and in her second career as a corporate Human Resource Officer, she and her family are living in North Carolina. She states that "Dad believed in reading widely, and writing (he loved to write poetry), and he loved a good debate with family members and others about religion, politics, or anything that kept the mind active."

Retired Army First Sergeant Lynn Burns, now of Arizona recalls his dad encouraging him and his siblings by saying "you may not be able to achieve perfection, but you can achieve excellence." He recalls being taught to "pay attention to details" and to always have a "plan B, and a plan C" to achieve your objectives.

Daughter, Nedra, also a corporate Human Resources Officer, and her family live in Fulton County. She states that "he did not have a booming voice, but he had a quiet presence that commanded respect." She goes on to say that "he discouraged gossip and encouraged everyone he touched to see the good in others. He reached out to those in need and he gave to those who were without."

In and beyond the walls of the church, he loved working with the youth and guiding their development. There is a consensus in the Burns family that their dad believed that failure was not an option. Darryl (now deceased), Margo and Yvonne were raised in the Burns home and were beneficiaries of the same love, discipline and encouragement received by all the children. Rev. Burns regularly reached out to young people and encouraged and challenged them to set high goals in life and to pursue them.

Mrs. Addie Burns is so thankful that God gave her a loving, caring, and God-fearing husband and father of their children. She is thankful for the example he set in their home, in the community and in his career as a military man and as a minister of the gospel of Jesus Christ. Indeed, he lived out his ministry calling with the same high level of commitment and energy as he served in the military. Over the years, he served as pastor of Mount Calvary Baptist Church in Elberton, St. Marlenes, Macedonia, and New Sutton Temple.

As his ministry evolved, Rev. Burns discovered that God had given him a special love for elderly people. Accordingly, he began working with a fellow community-minded Washingtonian, Mary Ferguson in the early 1980s to begin a senior citizen program. It began operating modestly in the community service building of the Harper Street housing development in December 1981.

In 1982 and for the ensuing ten years, the Senior Citizens Center operated out of the old Reese J. Booker Recreational Center on Whitehall Street. When the need to expand arose, Rev. Burns began exploring the availability of grant money and other resources to build and staff a new facility. The new Wilkes County Senior Citizens Center was constructed several years ago at a cost of about $400,000 and was financed principally by a Community Development Block Grant from the Georgia Department of Human Resources.

To honor the life, hard work and dedication of Rev. Burns in making the center a reality, it was in 2009 renamed, the Roy L. Burns, Sr. Senior Citizen Center. Like church and family, it has great significance in the lives of a huge number of our seniors each day.

"The Senior Citizens Center is a tremendous plus to the quality of life for the seniors in Washington and Wilkes County" says Mayor Willie Burns. "I am so elated that God put it in my dad's spirit to work to make it a reality. His life was about service – to God, family, country, and especially Wilkes County." Indeed, Rev. Roy L. Burns, Sr. is an **Unsung Hero of Wilkes County**.

PART TWO

Education Leaders

"Ask, and it will be given to you; seek and you will find; knock, and it will be opened to you."

Matthew 7:7

"Nothing great in the world has been accomplished without passion."

G. W. Hegel – From Philosophy of History

"A man can fail many times, but he isn't a failure until he begins to blame somebody else."

John Burroughs

Chapter 9

PROFESSOR JOHN HENRY JACKSON
1903-1977

Education is the key to success
(February 2007)

Distinguished African American Educator, "Professor" John Henry Jackson was born May 1, 1903 in Wilkes County, GA to Charlie and Hattie Bonner Jackson. His mother was a school teacher at Third Shiloh Academy. After attending and graduating from the public schools of Washington, Georgia, he successfully earned a Bachelor of Science degree in education from Morehouse College of Atlanta, Georgia in 1927, during the presidency of the eminent educator and scholar, Dr. John Hope.

With degree in hand he returned to Wilkes County with a calling to uplift his people through education and at the same time provide the best possible care for his ailing mother who had inspired him to become an educator. After a period with the Civilian Conservation Corps (CCC), he began his teaching career in Lincoln County, GA. Around 1939, he accepted the position of teacher and Principal of New Ford Baptist Church Junior High and

Elementary School. His arrival at New Ford made it the only school in Northeast Wilkes County that provided education beyond the 7th grade to African American children in that quadrant of the county.

It was because of the energetic efforts of New Ford pastor and "Morehouse Man", Rev. Albert T. Zellars; World War 1 decorated veteran and school Trustee, Deacon Willie Cofer; church servant-leaders like Deacon Charlie Cofer, Deacon J. C. Brewer, Deacon Cap Robinson, Deacon Bradley, Trustee John Benson, and others working in harmony with the then County School Superintendent, Mr. W. T. Callaway, that New Ford was able to establish a junior high school and gain the services of "Professor" Jackson, who was at the time the only African American male teacher in the county with a college degree.

The best efforts of these men could not persuade the county to provide bus transportation to students of color in the 1930's and 40's. Since the parents of most of the students were sharecroppers, there were very few families with cars. Accordingly, junior high school students would have to walk up to six or seven miles to school. In the case of three junior high school students, Ethel Mae Anderson (Johnson), Carrie Hudson (Gresham) (Mays), and Veola Cofer (Anderson) who lived in the Sandtown Community (5 miles from New Ford), "Professor" Jackson and his wife Mrs. Hattie M. Walton Jackson, who was an elementary school teacher at New Ford, would have them meet each day at the home of Reeves Chapel Baptist Church Deacon, Roy and Ethel Anderson (parents of Ethel Mae Anderson).

The Jacksons would lovingly stop each day, pick them up, and give them a ride to school. They would drop them off at Deacon Anderson's home after school in time for them to walk the remaining distance and get home in time to do their farm chores before it became dark. This continued over a three year period without the students or their families incurring any transportation costs.

Early on, "Professor" Jackson established himself as an outstanding math and history teacher and as a strict disciplinarian, who through tough love techniques, insisted on his students meeting academic and disciplinary high expectations. A large majority of his students responded to the challenge and have gone on to have successful careers and they have inspired their children and grandchildren to pursue college degrees and beyond, in many cases. His positive impact on New Ford students was such that some parents favored their children having to find a way to follow him from New Ford and the Danburg Community to the Rosenwald School (Black Rock) in Tignall, when he was transferred there in 1944.

Oldest son of "Professor" Jackson, John Jackson, recalls that his father instilled in each of his children a strong sense of pride. He states that they were taught to believe in themselves and to have a goal in life. A military war veteran and college graduate, John has had a rewarding career in the textile industry. Like his father, he and all his brothers – Booker, Charles, and Andrew - are active and lifelong members of Springfield Baptist Church, where their dad served for years as the Sunday School teacher for the adult class and Chairman of the Trustee Board.

John further recalls the deep commitment his father had to spending time in the evening and night, after a long day's work, teaching math and other academic skills under the GED program to military veterans.

Booker recalls that during the era of segregation, his father did not have the luxury of having an assistant principal, secretary, or other needed support personnel. The Jackson children and others were called on to assist with chores during the lunch period and at other times of the day. Booker recalls spending many days on the family's old Underwood typewriter typing the school menu and other matters for his dad. Now retired from the Wilkes County School System, he has had a very successful career as an educator. He has fond memories of his father as one who loved to play checkers and listen to the baseball game and Saturday night boxing matches with his family or the men of the community.

In her February 3, 1994 article entitled "*Educator Jackson seen as demanding, yet tolerant",* Patricia Wilder writes that "Jackson served as sole administrator of a school that included grades 1 – 12 and boosted an enrollment of some 1,200 students. Besides being administrator and chief disciplinarian with no clerical help, he also assumed many other duties that included bookkeeping and collecting lunch tickets at lunch time." She goes on to say "An avid believer in developing students to their fullest potential he was influential in starting both a football team and a band during his tenure." And lastly, she states that "Despite the limited resources, many graduates went on to become teachers, ministers, doctors, lawyers, and other productive members of society."

Charles Jackson remembers that his dad was a good father and family man. He concurs that he was a strict disciplinarian and a tough taskmaster who would constantly remind his children and his students that "education is the key to success." Charles has a deep appreciation for the role his dad played in the lives of so many young African American students of Wilkes County. He recalls a fairly recent letter he received from a former Wilkes Countian, Horace More, Ph.D. presently of California, who wrote simply to say that he is eternally grateful for having had Mr. Jackson for a teacher, mentor and role model. Dr. More expressed deep appreciation for the guidance and advice he received from Mr. Jackson while attempting to select the right college to attend.

The youngest son of "Professor" Jackson, Andrew, recently announced his retirement from Wilkes County Public Schools and the position of Principal, Washington-Wilkes Comprehensive High School, after a career that has spanned 34 years. He remembers his father as an avid historian, mathematician and disciplinarian. Andrew has the deepest respect for his father's experience as a high school principal during the era of segregation and he is humbled and honored to have been the first African American principal of the high school since integration. He knows that his dad is looking down and smiling at the achievements of the high school during his tenure as principal.

Because they live out of town, the opportunity was not there to interview the daughters of "Professor" John Henry Jackson. Marie Jackson Lane lives in Florida and is a very successful educator. Barbara Alexander is a very successful real estate broker and she is the first lady of one of Atlanta's largest and most revered Baptist churches.

Deacon Eddie Finnell first met "Professor" Jackson as a student in grade school, and was later in his adult Sunday School class at Springfield, and of course, was influenced by him and his protégés in the Wilkes County School System. Sounding much like Mr. Jackson's sons, Mr. Finnell describes Mr. Jackson as being well learned in mathematics and history and as a stern and strict disciplinarian who knew practically every child and their parents. He recalls Mr. Jackson as being a man who believed that everyone should be on time with following through with his/her commitments.

Proteges or mentees of Jackson who influenced Deacon Finnell and many present day teachers are such notable educators and community leaders as Mr. Reese J. Booker, Mrs. Rosa Warthen, Mr. Willie McLendon, Mrs. E. T. Bell, Mrs. Sarah Jones Marsh, Mr. John Hill, and many others who are giants in the field of education.

Washington and Wilkes County and its sons and daughters are in a better place in life because "Professor" John Henry Jackson passed our way. We thank God for him. He is gone, but he will never be forgotten. Indeed, he is an Unsung Hero of Wilkes County.

Chapter 10

MRS. OREE DEE WILLIS

A lifetime filled with love of learning and teaching
(February 2008)

Distinguished African American educator, Mrs. Oree Dee Willis was born March 22, 1922 in Grady Hospital in Atlanta, Georgia. Her parents, George Bennie Willis and Sarah Strickling Willis had moved from Wilkes County to Atlanta for a brief period. Shortly after her birth, they moved to Knoxville, Tennessee to join other family and church members and to seek employment.

When Mrs. Oree Dee was six years old, her parents separated and she was brought back to Wilkes County to grow up in the home of her maternal grandmother, Mrs. Mary Smith Stribling, along with four other cousins and four aunts and uncles. Her Grandma Mary was a midwife. She delivered hundreds of African American babies in the Tignall, Delhi, Sandtown, Danburg, and Washington communities in the 1930's, 40's and 50's including the writer of this article. Moreover, she provided home health care for scores of white mothers who had just given birth.

Mrs. Oree Dee discovered very early in life that she loved to learn. Even though the few books she and her classmates had at Pole Branch Baptist Church Elementary School were "hand me down" books from the white school in Tignall, she cherished them and absorbed every detail of every text book that was available to her. By the time she was in the second grade, Mrs. Oree Dee had purposed in her heart that she would be a school teacher. She especially enjoyed attending Pole Branch Church School from first through ninth grade. It was located next to her home church, Pole Branch Baptist Church and was the ancestral church of her father's side of the family.

Both the church and school had been founded by her great grandfather, Albert Willis, his sons and daughters and their families, and other African American men and women in the community. Her Grandpa Scott Willis and his brothers , Andrew Jackson, Will, Jonas, and others had, with their own hands, built the church and school she loved so much. She would go on to be a lifelong member of Pole Branch. Among the members of the church and school who positively influenced her was the church pastor, Rev. H. H. Hunter.

Rev. E. R. McLendon replaced Rev. Hunter and he continued to encourage her and all the students to get all the education they could get, to use their heads, and to grow up and "be somebody." Rev. E. R. McLendon was the son of Rev. Toombs McLendon, Sr. who had been the first pastor of Pole Branch. Rev. E. R. McLendon's mother was related to Mrs. Oree Dee in that Toombs, Sr. had married Fannie Willis, daughter of Mrs. Oree Dee's great grandfather, Albert Willis.

Others who encouraged and positively influenced Mrs. Oree Dee during her formative years were her teachers Mrs. Mary Smith and Mrs. Minnie Lee Willis. Mrs. Minnie Lee was married to Rev. James Walter "Son" Willis who was Mrs. Oree Dee's father's first cousin. She really felt supported and challenged at Pole Branch Church School. The concept of "it takes a village to raise a child" was alive and well with her. She and all her classmates, especially the Willis children, were expected to study hard and to do well.

Success stories about her late Great Grandfather Albert Willis also inspired Mrs. Oree Dee. He had been born in 1834 in the shadows of Monticello, the Charlottesville, Virginia, home of Thomas Jefferson, who had died in 1826. Albert Willis had been sold away from his mother for $1,000.00 into slavery in 1845, when he was eleven years old to James Henry Willis, a large plantation owner in Delhi, Wilkes County, Georgia, whose family was formerly from the Charlottesville, Virginia area.

Even as a young man, Grandpa Albert was a talented wood carver, as was his fellow Charlottesville native, Eston Hemings, son of enslaved Sally Hemings and President Thomas Jefferson. Such was the Willis family's high regard for the wood carving talent of Great Grandpa Albert that he was entrusted to delicately carve out the mantle above the fireplace in the James Henry Willis homehouse (Great Oaks) – a mantle that remains functional and decorative to this very day.

In a conversation I had with Mrs. Mary Sale Stennett, granddaughter of James Henry Willis, in the mid 1970's, she stated (with tears in her eyes) that all the Willis family loved Great Grandpa Albert and that he was extremely talented as a wood carver. Now owned by an Atlanta medical doctor, the Willis Plantation homehouse where Great Grandpa Albert grew up still stands on Delhi Road.

The 1860 and 1880 Federal Census lists Great Grandpa Albert's racial classification as "mulatto" which indicated that he had a white father. In the James Henry Willis household he was first a house servant, then the personal servant of James Henry Willis. He was allowed to learn to read and write. In 1861 when forty-one year old James Henry Willis (who was married with several children) volunteered for military service with the Delhi Rangers Volunteer Company, 15th Georgia Infantry, then 26 year old, Great Grandpa Albert (who was married to Ann Brewer Willis with two children, Harriett and Albert Willis, Jr.) was required to accompany him to fight in the Battle of Bull Run in Virginia.

James Henry Willis contracted measles (a potentially deadly disease at the time), and was taken by Great Grandpa Albert to the medical facility in, of all places, Charlottesville, Virginia to recuperate. Confederate War Records indicate that he continued to serve in that medical facility after his cure, until his discharge in November 1861. It can be assumed that both men interacted with family and friends during their fairly lengthy stay in their home town of Charlottesville. Great Grandpa Albert personally escorted James Henry back to Delhi, Wilkes County, GA when he was well enough to travel.

Perhaps the outcome of the war could be forseen by the two men and perhaps they agreed on a contract for mutual and peaceful existence in Wilkes County. Perhaps their bond included a blood relationship. What is known is that the survivors of the two men have shown respect and friendship toward one another for generations and that James Henry Willis enabled the purchase of some of his property by Great Grandpa Albert for farming purposes and for a family and community church for members who, like Great Grandpa Albert, chose to withdraw their letters from Beulah Baptist, to establish a church of their own.

The church they initially established, Trinity Baptist Church, still conducts worship services today. The above and other stories about Great Grandpa Albert Willis were a source of inspiration for Mrs. Oree Dee Willis in her youth.

Mrs. Oree Dee's thirst for education continued after grade school. She attended high school at Washington High School where she was encouraged by outstanding teachers like Mrs. Louise Wood and Mrs. Essie Bell. It was not until high school that her name became "Oree Dee." Her mom, like several other parents of that era, both black and white, had simply given her initials for a name.

The faculty and administration urged her and her family to have the initials which were given to her "R. D." become a name. Her family decided that R. D. would be formally named Oree Dee Willis. Immediately after her 1941 high school graduation, Mrs. Oree Dee felt compelled to continue preparation for her "calling" to become a teacher. She entered the intense two-year teacher training program of Albany State College in Albany, Georgia. Her family had no money, so entry into college and the job market were synonomous.

Fortunately, a job in the school cafeteria became available. It was an answer to prayer. Her sister, Florida would send what she could in that she was now working in Greenville, S. C. Realizing her daughter's irrepressible calling to be a teacher, her mother continued to work in Knoxville, TN and would regularly send money from her meager income.

Mrs. Oree Dee completed the intense teacher training program and returned to her beloved Wilkes County to begin her quest to further educate her family and fellow citizens. She was hired to teach at the Rosenwald School at Black Rock AME Church. After two years, the opportunity to teach at her beloved alma mater, Pole Branch Church School, became available and she eagerly accepted.

Mrs. Oree Dee would go on to teach at Wynn Chapel Church School until the opportunity presented itself to enroll in the newly created four-year teacher training program at Albany State University. With two years already under her belt, she earned her BA degree in education in 1951.

Again, she anxiously returned to her beloved Wilkes County, for she was committed to the uplift of her people in her home county. For the ensuing nineteen years she passionately taught at New Ford Church School and North Wilkes Elementary School. A believer in lifelong learning, Mrs. Oree Dee spent summers during these working years enrolled in graduate and staff development courses at Johnson C. Smith University, Florida State University, Penn State University and The University of Georgia.

Moreover, she taught Language Arts at Washington High School during the period 1970 until 1977. Her hard work, commitment to teaching and continued academic development enabled her to complete the requirements for the degree, Master of Arts in Elementary Education in 1975 from The University of Georgia. Additionally, she had earned enough credits to be awarded a Certificate in Educational Administration from UGA.

In 1977, Mrs. Oree Dee was asked to come serve at the Board of Education Central Office as the first African American to administer the Federal Title 1 program. A lifelong classroom teacher, she prayed about the offer and decided that it would indeed be an opportunity to help a greater number of youngsters in the entire CSRA achieve their educational objectives. While the classroom was her first love, she states that she received a greater sense of gratification in helping students and their families on a larger scale.

By accepting and serving in the position, Mrs. Oree Dee became the first person of color to serve on the Wilkes County Board of Education central staff. Mrs. Oree Dee retired from Wilkes County Public School System in 1986 after more than four decades of honorable and committed service to the children of Wilkes County and the CSRA. She credits God for granting her the opportunity to live out His calling for her life.

Rufus Willis (no relation) married Oree Dee Willis in 1945. She did not have to change her last name. She was blessed to have a husband who understood that teaching was a passion for his wife. He accepted her commitment to be academically qualified and to devote much time to her students.

Two children were born to Mr. and Mrs. Rufus Willis, but one died during infancy. Their daughter, Deborah Willis Mays and her family live in Riverdale, GA. Mrs. Oree Dee has three granddaughters and will soon be a great grandmother. Her husband, Rufus went home to be with the Lord in 1987.

Mrs. Oree Dee was and is still quite active in her church, Pole Branch Baptist Church, as well. She accepted Christ as her personal Savior in her youth and has been a tireless and committed Christian throughout her adult life. Over the years, she has served as Church Secretary for 32 years, Vacation Bible School Director for 40 years, Adult Sunday School teacher for 20 years, and member of the Trustee Ministry for 12 years. Mrs. Oree Dee loves her church and she loves the Lord.

Looking back on her life and career, she is grateful to God for giving her a very rich and satisfying life filled with family, friends, love ones, a career doing what she feels she was "called" to do, a church and church family, and the gift of everlasting life.

Her greatest regret is that the "powers that be" took prayer out of the public schools and restricted the use of corporal punishment. Mrs. Oree Dee cherishes her former colleagues, former students, and all of God's family. She now devotes her time to Pole Branch Baptist Church, her family (she is the Historian for the Willis Family Reunion), and several of her favorite charities. Mrs. Oree Dee Willis' roots run deep in Wilkes County. Indeed, she is an authentic Unsung Hero of Wilkes County.

Chapter 11

ARTHUR W. "DOC" DANNER

I, too, can be successful and determination pays off February, 2013

Distinguished African American retired College Administrator, Arthur Watson "Doc" Danner was born to Thomas and Anna Aplin-Brewer-Danner on March 28, 1933 on Third Street near the old Stockyard in Wilkes County, Georgia. Shortly after his birth, his mother was hospitalized with acute pulmonary tuberculosis. The disease required that she be separated from her family.

At age six months, Arthur and two of his four sisters, Reber and Lena, were taken into the care of their paternal grandparents, Alex and Lillie Danner. His other two sisters, Louise and Anna were placed in the care of their paternal grandparents, Simon and Lucy Brewer. The health of Arthur's mother deteriorated rapidly and sadly, she passed when he was eighteen months old.

Arthur's grandparents struggled with the rigors of sharecropping in the Danburg Community. This meant, in part, that as a young lad, Arthur had multiple chores to perform prior to his near two mile walk to New Ford Church School in the morning, and additional chores upon his afternoon near two mile trek back home. Early on, he determined that he loved school, in spite of the long walk he and his black friends experienced while the white kids rode pass them on buses. He decided to develop his mind and thereby escape the hard life experienced by his hardworking, loving, church-going, Christian, but forever financially challenged sharecropping grandparents.

After grades one through eight at New Ford Church School under the tutelage of Mrs. Hattie Jackson, Mrs. Lois Nash and others, Arthur followed fellow Danburg community high school student, Gartrell Robinson and transferred to Rosenwald High School in Tignall, Georgia where Professor Clarence Andrews was the principal. He planted and harvested an extra acre of cotton to earn enough money to purchase a new Goodyear bicycle and pedaled the, then, dirt roads eight miles each way from Danburg to the school in Tignall to pursue his dream.

His grandparents sacrificed his presence on the farm to accommodate his determination to be successful. In 1950, Arthur overcame the farm life that consumed an overwhelmingly large percentage of young black students and he earned a coveted high school diploma. In fact, he was class Valedictorian. His pre-civil rights era desire to attend the University of Georgia was a non-starter so, with a $135.00 a year academic scholarship to Clark College in Atlanta and a commitment to work his way through college, he enrolled in Clark College in September 1950. That same year, he began employment as a service station attendant at Sears & Roebuck in Atlanta.

The ongoing Korean Conflict caused him to be drafted after completing three semesters at Clark. Rather than applying for an educational deferment, he chose to report for active duty and serve his country even if it meant risking serving on the front lines in a time of war. As it turned out he was assigned first to Fort Gordon, then to Japan. Arthur was honorably discharged in 1955. He returned to Atlanta, was married to his longtime sweetheart from Washington, Georgia, Vinnie Mae Coleman, and they began a family which ultimately increased to four children.

To support his family, he commenced working for North Carolina Mutual Life Insurance Company as an Insurance Salesman, then at Amorite Division, Anaconda Aluminum as a machine operator. With the G. I. Bill educational benefits in hand, he continued his studies at Clark in 1957. After earning his B.S. in Business Administration and Accounting in 1960, Arthur continued his studies and earned an MBA from Clark College with a concentration in Finance and Management in 1962.

Arthur's first college administrator assignment was in 1962 as the Business Manager and Assistant Professor at Philander Smith College in Little Rock, Arkansas. During the ensuing 34 years, he served as Chief Financial Officer at five different colleges culminating in his service as Vice President for Finance and Budget during the last 16 years of his illustrious career at University of the District of Columbia (UDC) in Washington, DC.

At the time of his retirement, University of the District of Columbia had an annual operating budget of 85 million dollars and an enrollment of 7,500 students. His primary fiduciary responsibilities as the Chief Financial Officer were to oversee the management, accounting, internal controls, and financial reporting of funds received and used by the universities as authorized by their respective Boards of Trustees.

He has received numerous awards and recognitions for his many years of professional service.

Since his 1996 retirement, Arthur has endeavored to contribute to his family, his church and his community in any way that he can. Through his writing, he has attempted to enlighten fellow citizens in order to inspire them to achieve their highest potential. He has attempted to assist at the city government level. For several years he has served as the Adult Sunday School teacher at his beloved Mulberry Baptist Church. With diminishing eye sight, he has had to yield his teaching responsibilities to others. Nevertheless, he is faithful in his attendance and participation as a student and worshipper in the church of his youth. With much love, gratitude, and humility, he continues to thank God for His goodness in his life.

Arthur married Shelia Blalock during his tenure at UDC. He has co-parented ten children, eight of whom are independent adults and college graduates. Among them are a lawyer, doctor, minister, two certified public accountants, law enforcement officer, and members of corporate America. The remaining two children are still in college. He is the grandfather of ten and the great-grandfather of five. He has the confidence of knowing that his hard work and sacrifices were instrumental in providing the foundation for success in the form of security, education, economics, spiritual and social development to propel his posterity into the middle class.

Now a resident of Lincolnton, Georgia, he enjoys regular fellowship with his beloved sister, Reber. He looks forward to calls and visits from other members of his family, and he is actively involved at Mulberry Baptist Church. His special friend, Professor Barbara Carter of Spellman College in Atlanta, Georgia, is a source of inspiration, intellectual stimulation, and comfort to him as he enters his eighth decade of life.

"Doc" Danner has inspired so many in his family, his community, and in his profession with his quest to overcome adversity and with his remarkable and successful career. We wish him well and congratulate him on overcoming the odds and achieving great success. He is unquestionably one of the great Unsung Heroes of Wilkes County, Georgia.

PART THREE

Business Leaders

"For God so loved the world that He gave His only begotten son that whosoever believes in Him shall not perish, but have everlasting life."

John 3:16

"He who does not have the church as his mother does not have God as his father."

Saint Augustine

"The church must be reminded that it is not the master or the servant of the state, but rather the conscience of the state."

Martin Luther King, Jr.

Chapter 12

BESSIE WELLMAKER MCLENDON

She was an anchor for the funeral home for three generations (February, 2007)

Distinguished African American businesswoman and funeral home director, Bessie Wellmaker McLendon was born March 28, 1916 in the Metasville Community of Wilkes County, Georgia. She is the youngest of two children born to Isaiah and Addie Moman Wellmaker. She is 18 years younger than her sister, Emmie who married Fleming Turman.

Ms. Bessie has vivid and fond memories of her maternal grandmother, Lizzie Paschal Moman, who was of pure African heritage, and her maternal grandfather, who was a Native American Indian with long flowing black hair. Ms. Bessie's father, Isaiah was the son of a German immigrant (Jack Wellmaker) and Amelia, an African American lady. Her father was a miner until he lost both hands in a mining accident in McDuffie County.

With his modest savings and with the help of his father, Jack, Isaiah bought a farm and hired men to do the work, therefore enabling him to adequately provide for his family until his untimely death at age 57.

Ms. Bessie was educated in the public/church schools of Lincoln and Wilkes County. She pleasantly recalls her first teacher at Harmony Church Elementary School, Mrs. Ella Ware, and she remembers the school at Mt. Nebo Baptist Church and her teacher, Mrs. Sallie Walton. The distance from her house to each school was about four miles. Just getting to school was a major challenge since the county provided bus transportation to white students but not to African American students.

Roads were often not paved and not very well kept up, she recalls. When it rained hard or flooded the children would have to "make haste" to cross the bridge or they would get stranded overnight. This happened to Ms. Bessie on one occasion in the mid 1920s and she had to spend the night at the home of Mrs. Marie Walton. There were no cars or telephones in the African American community, so parents whose children did not safely arrive at home from school after a heavy rain could only pray and endure sleepless nights trusting that a community member on the school side of the bridge had taken their child in for the night. By the grace of God, the children either made it home or were taken care of by good neighbors every time.

In 1933, at age 17, Ms. Bessie married Toombs McLendon, Jr. son of successful businessman and pastor of Mt. Carmel Baptist Church, Toombs McLendon, Sr. In his book entitled *THE HISTORY OF WILKES COUNTY, GEORGIA,* Robert M. Willingham, Jr. writes, "Toombs McLendon, a remarkably astute and energetic young businessman opened McLendon's Funeral Home in 1883, becoming the second black funeral director in Georgia.

Willingham goes on to say that Rev. Toombs McLendon erected a large ginnery on his land in Baltimore and was opened by September 1, 1908." Toombs, Sr. was involved in other business ventures, as well. Clearly, the McLendon family had an entrepreneurial or business spirit from early times. At the time of their 1933 marriage, Toombs, Jr. was already a successful business man in his own right.

In 1934, their daughter Norris was born and two years later Toombs, the 3d was born. Ms. Bessie's husband immediately began to teach her how to function as part of the funeral home business. He quickly realized that she was quite talented and had good business savvy.

Over a period of 74 years (three generations) she has provided a strong arm of love, support, and advice to her husband, her son, and now to her grandson, Toombs, the 4th. With her husband having passed in 1957 and her son in 1984, she and her grandson, Toombs, the 4th still take pride in serving the people of Wilkes and surrounding counties with the best possible mortuary services available. McLendon Memorial Funeral Home is not just one of the oldest and most respected businesses in the African American community, it is one of the oldest and most respected businesses throughout Wilkes County, Georgia.

It is that rare example of the next generation stepping up to carry on the business founded by the foreparents. Countless thousands of families have for generations relied on Ms. Bessie and Toombs to serve their family in their time of greatest need. There are many children who have been told by their parents for years "when my time comes, I want Bessie to have my body." McLendon Memorial Funeral Home still commands a high level of confidence in the community and county.

In recalling some of the larger and most memorable funerals arranged during her many years of serving the community, Ms. Bessie points out that every funeral is equally important and must be carried out with dignity, good order, and professionalism. The funerals of her husband and son were especially difficult and overwhelming. She recalls that the funeral of one of Wilkes County's great preachers, Rev. Charles Turman, was one of the largest and most challenging to coordinate.

In addition to providing employment to scores of people over the years, she and her husband have served as mentors and trainers for young men desiring to have a career in the funeral home business. Three such young men are the sons of Rev. James Walter and Minnie Lee Willis; Marion, Jonas, and William James. Each received additional formal training in mortuary science after leaving Wilkes County and each have had full careers in the funeral home business.

The late Marion Willis established and operated a funeral home in Detroit, Michigan. The late Jonas Willis spent a lifetime in the career field in Santa Monica, California. William James "Willie James" Willis established a very lucrative funeral home business in Dalton, Georgia with branches in several surrounding towns. Now semi-retired, his son, wife, daughters, and sister keep quite busy serving the needs of bereaved families in a large portion of the North Georgia community.

Ms. Bessie prides herself in having been, perhaps the very first African American female ambulance driver in the county. During the era of segregation, she would use the funeral home hearse and other vehicles to deliver the sick and injured to and from the hospital in Washington and often to and from the hospital in Augusta. Often, appropriate compensation was not forthcoming, but she found gratification in helping the sick and afflicted get the needed medical care.

As she reflects on her life as a person who could operate on either side of the color line, she acknowledges that she used all the advantages God gave her to achieve success for her family and business.

A Seventh-Day Adventist, she gives God the credit for sustaining her during a life of ups and downs, triumphs and defeats, successes and failures. Now retired, she offers whatever assistance she can to the operation of the funeral home. She enjoys hearing from her daughter, grandchildren, and eight great-grandchildren.

Ms. Bessie has positively touched the lives of thousands of Wilkes Countians and others during her 74 years in the funeral home business and her almost 91 years of life. She has been a pacesetter, a role model, a pioneer, an astute business woman, a friend, and an authentic unsung hero in Wilkes County, Georgia.

Chapter 13

WILLIAM JAMES WILLIS, SR.

Well grounded in the Word, Willis is one of the Greatest Generation (February, 2010)

Distinguished African American Mortician and Funeral Home Director, William James Willis, Sr. was born April 30, 1924 in Tignall, Georgia to the late Reverend James Walter "Son" Willis (1896 - 1973) and Mrs. Minnie Lee Andrews Willis (1900 - 1971).

His paternal grandparents are Deacon Andrew Jackson (1870 - 1918) and Lula Bell Hill Willis (1873 -1949) of Tignall, Georgia. His paternal great grandparents are Deacon Albert (1834-1919) and Ann Willis (1836 - 1926) of Tignall, Georgia. His maternal grandparents are William (18?-1930) and Kathryn Cade Andrews (18?-1938) of Tignall, Georgia.

He has been united in Holy Matrimony to Dorothy Sprowl Willis for 62 years and they are the parents of three wonderful and successful children. In naming their children, they followed an old tradition in the black community which has its history in the African tradition of naming a newborn child after one of the elders in the community who is/was loved and respected by the parents of the newborn baby.

Their oldest child, William James "Jimmy" Willis, Jr. (married to Joyce Harding Willis) is named after his father. William James, Sr. was originally named Willie James, but officially changed his name while in high school. Their second child, Minnie Ruth Willis Marsh (married to Hubert Andrew Marsh, Sr.) bears the first name of her paternal grandmother and the middle name of her maternal grandmother. Their third child, Mary Lee Willis Suttles (married to Dony Suttles) bears the first name of her maternal grandmother and the middle name of her paternal grandmother. William James and Dorothy Sprowl Willis are the proud grandparents of seven grandchildren, Willisa H. Marsh, Hubert Andrew (Andy) Marsh, Jr.(married to Frances), Joycelyn Y. Willis, Juanita E. Willis(married to Craig Hicks), Daryll Tinson, Derrick Tinson, and Daniel Tinson. They are the proud great grandparents of William L. Hicks and Andrea Electa Marsh.

With a father who was a farmer and a Baptist Preacher and a mother who was a school teacher, Willie James and his younger siblings, Jonas, Marion, and Geri, each day began and ended with fervent family prayer in the Willis household. After breakfast and chores, it was off to school. Usually, the children attended the one or two room rural schools where their mother taught school. This enabled her to parent, inspire, teach and monitor them throughout the day.

Mrs. Willis had William James accompany his ailing Grandmother Kathryn Cade to Dalton, Georgia when he was a young teenager. An avid learner, he liked Dalton and the educational opportunities it provided. In Wilkes County, black students had a different school year than the white students.

School for black students began in October, after they and their parents had picked all the cotton.

In Dalton, he was able to begin school around Labor Day and complete the same full school year as the white kids. His middle and high schools in Dalton were segregated in the 1930's and 40s, for indeed, this was long before the U. S. Supreme Court handed down its 1954 decision in the landmark case, Brown v. Board of Education declaring that segregation in public schools is inherently unequal and decreeing that public schools were to be integrated "with all deliberate speed." It would be difficult for Rev. "Son" Willis, the "walking preacher", to do without his oldest son's help on the family farm on Delhi Road, but God gave him and his wife the desire to see that their children have a better opportunity in life than they had.

Reluctantly, they listened to their son's request to be allowed to remain in Dalton and attend school. They were aware that there were limited educational opportunities past the 6th grade, one and two room schools for young African American students in Wilkes County. In Dalton, William James could be assured of the opportunity to finish high school. His parents understood the importance of getting a good education. He assured them that he would not let them down. He would work hard, pray hard, and write home regularly. They made the decision to give him the opportunity to succeed.

William James did not disappoint his parents. Throughout his life he has been grateful to them and to God for the opportunity he was provided. He would return to Wilkes County each summer to help his parents on the farm and to serve as an apprentice/intern at T. A. McLendon's Funeral Home.

One of his first school acquaintances in Dalton was an

intelligent and wonderful young lady who sat behind him in his middle school class room. Her name was Dorothy Sprowl. A friendship that began in their early teen years later evolved into a courtship, then marriage that has produced beautiful children, grandchildren, great grandchildren, a beautiful and loving home, an enduring and profitable family business, respect and standing in the church, community, county, and state, and in his profession. On his many return trips from Wilkes County during his teenage years, he would often speak to Dorothy with enthusiasm and passion about his desire to be a part of the funeral home industry.

In the pre-Civil Rights and Jim Crow era, William James had already discovered his calling. While opportunities were limited and social and economic conditions for blacks in Georgia and throughout the south were challenging, he had a clear vision of the future. For indeed, his home training, religious and secular education, and educated and God-fearing parents and grandparents gave him a strong self concept and the confidence that "he could do all things through Christ who strengthens him."

Well grounded in the Word of God, William James had accepted Christ at an early age at Pole Branch Baptist Church under the pastorate of Rev. Earl McLendon. He had seen the hand of God at work in his own life, and in the lives of his Godly parents, grandparents, great grandparents, fellow church members, and members of the community. He understood that he had a Godly heritage and that he was expected to work hard, study hard, pray hard, be humble and respectful, and do unto others as he would have them do unto him.

He understood that the torch was being passed to him and his generation from the patriarch and matriarch of the African American branch of the Willis family in Georgia, Deacon Albert Willis and his wife Ann Willis down through his grandparents,

Deacon Andrew Jackson and Lula Bell Hill Willis; on down through his parents, Rev. James Walter and Minnie Lee Andrews Willis . The Willis family patriarch, Albert Willis had been born in Charlottesville, Virginia in 1834 during that awful time in the history of the United States when human beings bought and sold and enslaved other human beings based on the color of their skin.

When Albert was eleven, his mother and four(?) siblings were sold to different plantation owners in other states. Young Albert was sold to wealthy Wilkes County plantation owner, James Henry Willis. A so-called mulatto, which means that one of his parents was white, young Albert required medical attention, no doubt, because of mental and physical aspects of his ordeal. He was assigned duties as a house servant on the Willis Plantation. During that time, it was discovered that this young man, who was born in the vicinity of Monticello, Virginia, had the same wood carving talent and skills as Eston Hemings, the son of Sallie Hemings and Thomas Jefferson of Monticello.

A mantle he carved somewhere between 1845 and 1919 is still a point of pride at "Great Oaks", the old Willis Plantation on Delhi Road, now owned by Mr. and Mrs. Barnett of Atlanta, Georgia. During Wilkes County's September 18, 2009 Fall Ramble sponsored by the Georgia Trust, many citizens and students of history marveled at this great work of art. Albert Willis became the trusted "man servant" of James Henry Willis. In 1860, then 26 year old Albert went with 41 year old James Henry Willis and the Delhi Rangers off to the Battle of Bull Run or the Battle of Manassas in Virginia. Still enslaved, his job was to ensure that food and clean clothing was available to James Henry.

When James Henry became ill, Albert took him to the Confederate Army Dispensary in, of all places, Charlottesville, Virginia and helped to provide medical care for him. Later that year, upon his medical discharge, Albert helped James Henry return to "Great Oaks" where both men had wives and children awaiting their return. The Willis family oral history tells us that the deep loyalty Albert had for James Henry was because of a blood relationship. What is known is that after the war ended the two men and their families continued to live in close proximity to each other in peace and harmony and their descendants still do so 'til this day.

We also know that after the passage of the 13th, 14th, and 15th Amendments to the United States Constitution, Albert and his family became the benefactors of land for their personal farming use and for the building of a family church, Trinity Baptist Church, which has stood as a beacon of light in the Delhi Community since 1880.

William James knew his history and his heritage. He knew that his great grandfather, Albert Willis had learned to read and write in spite of his enslaved status and went on to become a successful land owner, farmer, Pole Branch church deacon, and family man. He knew that his grandfather, Andrew Jackson Willis was literate, had helped build Pole Branch Baptist Church and Church School, was a church deacon, successful farmer and family man.

His own father was educated and had the confidence of the community as one of Wilkes County's most trusted and sincere ministers of the Gospel. William James knew that his mother had attended Paine College in Augusta, Georgia and was a superb school teacher. Indeed, this son, grandson, and great-grandson of a minister, teacher and deacons, respectively, understood that he had a Godly heritage and he accepted the charge to prepare himself for life and to pass his heritage on.

After his 1942 graduation from Emery Street High School in Dalton, Georgia, William James attended Morehouse College in Atlanta, Georgia with a view toward majoring in business in preparation for a career as a Funeral Home Director and Mortician. While in Atlanta he continued his quest to perfect his skills by apprenticing/interning at Andrews Funeral Home. While at Morehouse and in later years, he built a meaningful relationship with then Morehouse College President, Dr. Benjamin E. Mays who was also mentor to Dr. Martin Luther King Jr. William James states that Dr. Mays' mother, Carrie Mays and his mother, Minnie Lee had been classmates together at Paine College.

With World War ll at its peak, after receiving previous draft deferments, he was again drafted after completing his first year at Morehouse College. He chose to volunteer to serve his country in the United States Marine Corps in 1943. The rigorous and demanding life of the farm had prepared him for success in basic training at Camp LeJeune, North Carolina.

William James' high level of development of intellect and character enabled him to be selected for service in high level military administrative positions in Okinawa during the War. He personally and often interacted with General Jimmy Doolittle on a regular basis. He was in attendance and witnessed General Douglas McArthur's participation in the parade on Okinawa marking the signing of the Peace Treaty ending World War II.

His prior experience interning at funeral homes and his acceptance of the calling into the profession made William James sensitive to how the bodies of his fellow Marines and other service members were being handled. Most were buried in the combat zone. Upon being informed that after the war, many bodies would be exhumed and sent to the United States for burial at a location preferred by their families, he wrote the Army's Quartermaster General and informed him of his training, experience, concern, and career aspirations in the field of Mortuary Science. A return letter arriving in his military unit mailroom for Corporal William James Willis raised a few eyebrows and created concern that he had violated his chain of command.

His superiors were relieved to know that it was not a response to a serious complaint, but rather a response to William James' offer to make himself available in the post war effort to assist in preparing the bodies of his fallen fellow service members so they could be returned home to their families for burial. The Quartermaster General asked that he be kept informed of William James military status and address. He complied.

After his December 27, 1945 honorable discharge from the Marine Corps, William James immediately returned to Georgia and enrolled in the Atlanta College of Mortuary Science and he communicated that to the Office of the Quartermaster General. After 33 months of tough military duty, most of which was overseas in a combat zone, he was now ready to academically prepare for his life's work. Throughout his years away, he had stayed in touch, through cards, letters and mailgrams with his parents, siblings, aunts, uncles, friends, and most importantly, the young lady who had become his best friend in life, Dorothy Sprowl.

In 1947, he graduated from The Atlanta College of Mortuary Science and immediately passed the Georgia State Board of Embalming. Sure enough, the Graves Registration Branch of the Quartermasters Corps made him an immediate offer for civilian employment as the very first embalmer hired in the United States for graves registration duties after World War II. He was given a choice of service in the European Theater or the South Pacific Theater. He chose the South Pacific Theater which consisted of the Pacific Islands, Japan, Korea, Australia, and Okinawa, and he was ultimately based in Hawaii, with supervisory responsibility for the Pacific Theater of Operations.

Dean Pierce of the Atlanta College of Mortuary Science was so proud of the success of their new graduate that he posted William James' offer on the school official bulletin board. As a result, additional graduates of the college were able to begin their careers with important Graves Registration duties. Supervisor William James was empowered to hire 16 people. He hired eight blacks and eight whites to serve with him. Before departing for Hawaii and the Pacific Area, he respectfully requested a two week delay.

Now that he would soon have the financial means to support himself and a family it was time to ask for the hand in marriage of his closest friend and best supporter in life, Dorothy Sprowl. She had stood by him, encouraged him, written him during the war years, prayed for him, and loved him. He was the happiest man in the world when she said yes.

When they arrived in rural Wahuwa, Hawaii, they were down to their last sixty cents, but the future never seemed brighter because they were young, in love, and focused on their goals and objectives. During William James' service overseas, Dorothy had continued her preparation for a career as a registered nurse. She had earned her nursing credentials and was able to find immediate employment as the very first registered nurse in Wahuwa, Hawaii.

During those initial, critical months in Hawaii they struggled with housing, transportation, and other issues. But they stuck together and they continued to trust in God. A real blessing occurred when Dorothy was able to eat her meals at the hospital where she worked, at no cost to her and was allowed to have William James join her for the evening meal at no cost. Their two and a half years from 1947 to 1949 were challenging but most rewarding.

As Supervisor (embalmer/funeral director) of the primary United States sponsored operation designed to return all the war dead from throughout the Pacific Theater and the Far East, with honor and dignity, William James was pleased with his service and his achievement. The families of the deceased service members and the United States Government were quite pleased, as well. Among many other highlights to his service is the fact that he had been in charge of conducting the funeral of the first soldier buried in the National Memorial in Honolulu, Hawaii.

Many American Generals, Admirals, officers, Non-commissioned officers and regular service members are buried at the National Memorial. His name and the names of a few others who were present at the conception are inscribed on or near the flagpole at the entrance to that monument. Moreover, their first child, "Jimmy" had been born in Hawaii and now that the mission had been completed, it was time to return to Georgia.

At age 25, he and his wife established the Willis Funeral Home in Dalton, Georgia in 1949. For over sixty years, they, their three children, grandchildren and others have been a stable, caring and dependable family business serving Dalton and Northwest Georgia the old fashion way – "from the heart, and with a sincere desire to help one's fellow man." Periodically they are still called on to serve members of the Wilkes County community in their time of greatest need.

Throughout the years William James and his family have returned to Wilkes County for the biannual Willis Family reunion. As often as possible, he attends or maintains contact with his home church, Pole Branch Baptist Church in Tignall, Georgia. He is in regular contact with his Wilkes County beloved cousins, Cora Willis Andrews and her family, Porter Bee Willis Jones and her family, Joe Pearl Andrews Coleman and her family, Oree Dee Willis and her family, and many others.

William James and Dorothy, who is also a licensed funeral director, continue to be quite active in the operation of the funeral home. After many years in the nursing profession, Dorothy decided in 1966 that the time had come for her to dedicate herself to being a full time mom and helpmate to her husband in their rapidly growing family business. "What a blessing that has been to our family and our business" says William James.

Dorothy adds that her entire life with her best friend and her husband, their children and their spouses, their grandchildren and great grandchildren, the good friends, and the family business, has been a life of caring, committed, loving relationships with the best people in God's creation. She goes on to quote the gospel singer, "I won't take nothing for my journey now."

Wiliam James' only sister, Geraldine "Geri" Willis Pero, after several years of living in California near their brother, Jonas and his family (also in the funeral home business), joined the staff of the funeral home in the 1980s. From their days together in Wilkes County, she always knew that her big brother was going into the funeral home business. As a youngster, he had much empathy for deceased farm animals and would ensure that they were buried with respect.

Geri remembers that William James has always been a people person. He loves all members of the family and is the historian for the Andrews/Willis Family. Relatives gravitate to him because they enjoy him telling stories about family and events long since passed. The third of the Willis brothers was a career barber and raised his family in Detroit, Michigan.

For all intents and purposes, William James and Dorothy have passed the torch to the next generation. Their three children, Jimmy, Minnie Ruth, and Mary Lee, grew up in the business. Jimmy and Mary Lee are licensed funeral directors and embalmers. In addition to apprenticing in the funeral home as a young man, Jimmy is a graduate of Kentucky School of Mortuary Science.

Like his father, he gained extensive embalming and graves registration experience in the military. He served with distinction during the VietNam Conflict, ensuring that our war dead were properly attended to, with honor and dignity, and returned to the United States to a final resting place.

Bearing a very close physical resemblance to his father, he is leading this and the next generation of family members in their funeral home business with the same high level of care and professionalism established by his parents. He finds time to be a mentor to young men in the community. Jimmy is married to Joyce Harding Willis, who has had a rewarding career at the Dependent and Family Services. Their daughter, Juanita is a graduate of West Georgia College and is married to Craig Hicks and they have one son, William Lawyer Hicks. Jocelyn is a graduate of West Georgia College and is an educator.

Minnie Ruth (Mimi) earned an undergraduate degree and a Master of Arts in Education degree from Berry College. She has served as a successful educator in the Dalton Public Schools. In

1995 she was the first African American elected to the local Board of Education. She is a licensed insurance agent and puts her skills and training to work for the family funeral home. She and her husband, Hubert, are active members of Mt. Zion Baptist Church. Their daughter Willisa is a graduate of Berry College and is an educator. Their son Andrew attended Berkley College in Boston and is an educator. Mimi says, "my father is a person who has helped so many people in our community.

Beyond funeral services, he has served on many boards and in the church. I remember as a child that Daddy was busy with church work as the Church Clerk and member of the Usher Board and Deacon Board. As a young man, he was a Boy Scout troop leader. He always stressed that honesty and integrity are most important when in service to others. His motto for operating his business has been the Golden Rule, 'Do unto others as you would have them do unto you.'

I have been blessed to have the opportunity to work with my father in the family business; to learn from his wisdom, and to follow his example. I am so blessed to have him as my dad. For his grandchildren and great grandchildren, he is the most loving and caring grandfather."

Mary Lee is the youngest of the siblings and is a graduate of Cincinnati School of Mortuary Science and has earned her Bachelor of Arts degree in Business Administration from Berry College. She is a licensed youth minister at Liberty Baptist Church and is an accomplished wedding director, as well. Mary Lee says, "I thank God for my parents, my sister and brother. They were always so protective of me. My parents provided such a great example of caring for others and service to our church and community. To this very day I try, in my own life to follow their example.

One of my earlier positive images of my dad was watching him serve as an usher in our church. I decided early on that I, too, would be and usher. While I am involved in other areas of my church, I still serve, with great pride, as an usher. I remember daddy serving as a Boy Scout Leader and my brother serving as a Cub Scout Leader. Many of daddy's former scouts have gone on to become very successful men. I remember my mom allowing me to tag along and sit in the living room when she had to visit sick patients in their homes.

While I decided that I could not be a nurse, I developed a great admiration of her strength and compassion in caring for suffering people. I also admired the standard she set as the 'lady attendant' at funerals and I continue to work hard to regularly meet that high standard when called on." One of Mary Lee's three sons carried on the family tradition of military service. After completing a tour of duty in Iraq as a Marine, he attended and completed Atlanta Institute of Art. Son Daniel is a student at West Georgia College. Son Derrick is on a career path in the family business.

An ordained deacon, William James spent many years on the Liberty Street Baptist Church Deacon Board and as Church Clerk. Because of health and other family considerations, he is now a member of Hopewell Baptist Church in Dalton, Georgia. He is past president and past chairman of the executive board of the Georgia Funeral Service Practitioners Association, member of the National Funeral Directors and Morticians Association, Nu Epsilon Delta Mortuary Fraternity, past Vice President of the National Academy of Professional Funeral Service Practice, and past member of the Georgia Democratic Executive Committee.

He has chaired many boards in the community and county. He is past board member of the Dalton-Whitfield Chamber of Commerce, member of the Whitfield –Dalton Chapter of the

N.A.A.C.P. member of the Dalton Masonic Lodge No. 238, F & A.M. and Rome Consistory Lodge No. 264. He has been a friend and Advisor to former Governors Joe Frank Harris and Zell Miller. William James was named "Mortician of the Year" in 2003 by the 9th District of the Georgia Funeral Service Practitioners Association, Inc. He was awarded the Dalton Mayor's "Martin Luther King, Jr. Achievement Award" in 1990. He was inducted into the Dalton Education Foundation "Hall of Fame" in 1992 and he was named the Dalton-Whitfield Chamber of Commerce "Business Leader of the Year" in 1994.

In 1998, retired NBC news anchorman Tom Brokaw, in his book entitled *The Greatest Generation* wrote of his discovery of what those who fought in World War II mean to the history of America and the world. He calls these heroes and heroines the greatest generation any society has ever produced. He states that "they came of age during the Great Depression and the Second World War and went on to build modern America.

This generation was united not only by a common purpose, but also by common values – duty, honor, economy, country, and above all responsibility for oneself." While William James is not specifically mentioned in Brokaw's book, he certainly qualifies to have several chapters dedicated to his story. For indeed, he persevered in war, and when he returned home to America, he had to overcome segregation and a culture based on Jim Crowism. He and many others like him persevered and went on to create meaningful and useful lives and the America we have today. They raised their children to be overcomers in spite of adversity.

In addition to building a successful family business, which employs several others in the community, William James and Dorothy and their children and their spouses and offspring have clearly been contributing members to their community, county, city, state, and nation. They have been role models as husband and wife, parents, grandparents, and great-grandparents. They have been pace-setters, history makers, successful entrepreneurs, patriotic citizens, and Christian examples of a loving, caring and productive African American family.

Indeed, William James Willis is a distinguished "Unsung Hero of Wilkes County," and the rest of Georgia, as well.

Chapter 14

JOE L. ANDERSON, SR.

From the Sandtown Community to Corporate America (February 2013)

Distinguished African American corporate executive, retired Army Lieutenant Colonel, active religious leader and community volunteer, Joe Lewis Anderson was born in the Anderson Military District of Wilkes County in 1948, the third of nine children of Leroy and Veola Cofer Anderson who were sharecroppers at the time of his birth.

A six-generation descendant of Wilkes County, his ancestors include those who helped establish the following Wilkes County churches: Reeves Chapel, Mulberry, Fishing Creek, Cherry Grove, New Ford, Trinity and Pole Branch. His ancestors also include Native Americans who dwelled in Wilkes County prior to the "Trail of Tears."

The rigors of sharecropping were severe for Joe's family. In the 1950s they gave up farming and moved to Charlotte, NC, where his parents continued to instill in all their children a strong work ethic, a strong Christian faith, and a commitment to acquire all the education they could. Joe was an "A" student throughout Elementary School.

Prior to his eighth birthday, he along with his older brother took their first job selling a weekly newspaper, *The Charlotte Post.* Joe retained that job for about four years until he was old enough to have his own afternoon daily paper route with *The Charlotte News.* At age 14, he was promoted to Junior District Circulation Manager for *The Charlotte News* with responsibility to help develop younger newspaper carriers. At age 16, he was promoted to Relief District Manager by *The News* with responsibility to replace adult District Circulation Managers who were on vacation or ill.

Throughout Joe's entire childhood, each Sunday he and all his family attended Sunday school and morning worship services at New Hope Baptist Church, where he accepted Christ as his Lord and Savior at age 12. Always on the Honor Roll, he was a member of the Honor Society in Junior and Senior High School. He managed to find time to play on his high school tennis team where he was captain and number 1 player during his senior year.

At his high school graduation exercises, Joe was awarded the coveted "Civitan Good Citizenship Award", which is presented to the most "all around senior." He graduated with honors from West Charlotte Senior High School in Charlotte, NC and was awarded a partial academic scholarship to NC A & T State University in Greensboro, NC.

By that time, his parents had nine children, so it was necessary for him to continue to work in order to pay for the cost of college. While at A & T, Joe's serious pursuit of academics enabled him to be inducted into the Alpha Kappa Mu National Honor Society and Omicron Delta Epsilon Honor Society in Economics. He was also selected as a member of Who's Who among Students in American Colleges and Universities. In addition, he found the time to play on the college tennis team and to be an active part of the Army ROTC Program, where he was elected President of the Officer's Club.

During Joe's sophomore year at A&T, he also became a member of Omega Psi Phi Fraternity, a service organization that is now 100 years old that claims members such as Langston Hughes, Dr. Bill Cosby, Dr. Benjamin E. Mays, Michael Jordan and Dr. Ronald McNair (the astronaut who died in the Challenger accident). Of special note is that Dr. McNair became a member of the fraternity under Joe's tutelage while they were students at A&T.

In 1970, Joe graduated with honors (Cum Laude) with a Bachelor of Science degree in Economics and earned the designation Distinguished Military Graduate with a commission as a 2LT in the US Army Adjutant General Corps and was assigned to Fort Benning, Georgia. With orders to report for active duty in the spring 1971, he had about a year to begin his career in corporate America with Eastman Kodak Company of Rochester, NY where he was selected for the company's Management Training Program.

This also gave Joe time to plan his marriage to Angeles Webb, his childhood sweetheart who had graduated from A & T with him and was now a registered nurse in Washington, DC. They were married in August 1971. Kodak granted him a leave of absence to complete his two years of Vietnam Era active duty military service. While at Fort Benning, he was assigned as Adjutant of the post and his service earned him a promotion to First Lieutenant. Their first child, Joe, Jr. (a seventh generation Georgian) was born during Joe's assignment to Ft. Benning.

Joe and his family returned to Kodak in Rochester, NY in 1973 where his career as a Human Resources Manager began to blossom and his service in the military continued as an officer in the Army Reserves. Before long, son Jeffrey and daughter April were born. His career development path at Kodak facilitated Human Resources management assignments in the company's Mid-Atlantic Region headquartered in Arlington, VA., Western Region headquartered in San Francisco, CA. and corporate headquarters in Rochester, NY.

Joe played a key role at Eastman Kodak in the 70's and 80's, recruiting and hiring African Americans at Kodak's facilities across the nation while helping to develop and implement the company's diversity strategy throughout all of its operations. The result of his efforts was that Kodak received the coveted National Diversity Award as one of the best places in corporate America for minorities to work.

While at Kodak, he was also a founding member and Chairman of the Board of Network North Star, a network of African-American Professionals at Kodak. Additionally, he served as a founding member and first President of the Veterans Network of Kodak Employees (VETNET). There were 5,000 veterans employed by Kodak at the time of his leadership. He retired from Kodak in 2003 as a Senior Human Resources Manager with 33 years of service. Joe retired from the Army Reserves in 1996 as a Lieutenant Colonel after honorably serving in military units in New York, Maryland, New Jersey, and California.

JOE L. ANDERSON, SR. (Part 2)

"Christian Parenting + Great Education + Solid work ethic + Strong faith = Success"
(February, 2013)

Highly regarded African American Joe L. Anderson, Sr. has distinguished himself in corporate America, in the military, in the religious community, in his fraternity, and in the community at large.

He has served on numerous boards and advisory committees in the places where he has lived, including Action for a Better Community, Urban League of San Francisco, Baden Street Settlement, Hillside Family of Agencies, United Way of Greater Rochester, William Warfield Scholarship Fund, and Theta Omicron Scholarship Foundation. In addition, he is a member of the Executive Board of the Genesee Valley Chapter of the Military Officers Association of America (MOAA) and he is an officer in his hometown chapter of the American Legion.

After several years serving on the Board of Directors of Fairport Baptist Homes Caring Ministries, in 2011, Joe became the first African-American to be elected Chairman of the Board in the 107-year history of this organization. Fairport Baptist Homes Caring Ministries is a 24-million dollar organization comprised of a continuum of programs and services for seniors which include independent living, community care management, elder transportation, three different forms of assisted living, rehabilitative services, dementia care, resident-directed skilled nursing and an adult day health care facility.

In recognition of his decades of community service, Joe has previously been nominated to receive the Jefferson Award for Public Service, a prestigious national recognition system honoring community and public service in America.

A fiercely loyal and proud alumnus of NC A & T State University (the largest producer of Black engineers in the nation), Joe has served as Chairman of the Business and Industry Cluster, a group of 50 plus companies that support the university with scholarships and in other ways. University Chancellor, Harold L. Martin states, "Five years after his 1970 graduation from A & T, Joe established the Rochester NY Chapter of NC A & T Alumni Association and was elected its first president.

In his 33-year career at Eastman Kodak Company, Joe helped establish an employment pipeline from NC A & T to the company. He has provided the university more than $1 million in scholarships and other support. In 2010, the university's Board of Visitors was re-established and Joe was an obvious choice to be an inaugural member. He is a shining example of giving back and the entire A & T family is deeply grateful." As an expression of gratitude for his commitment to the university, A & T presented him with their Distinguished Service Award in 1996.

Rev. William Thomas, Associate Minister of Mount Vernon Baptist Church states that "Deacon Joe L. Anderson has been a faithful member of the Mt Vernon Missionary Baptist Church of Rochester, NY for nearly four decades. While standing firm on his faith, he generously donates his time and talents in many areas to include but not limited to The Deacons Ministry, the Layman Movement, Christian Education, and the New Members Committee.

He has made a positive impact within the church community by aiding in the process to develop young and new Christians into strong Bible believing saints. Words cannot express how blessed the Mt Vernon family is to have him." Moreover, Deacon Anderson is an active Vice President in the Empire Baptist Missionary Convention for the state of New York.

Joe is now a 44-year member of Omega Psi Phi Fraternity which is headquartered in Georgia where he presently serves as a member of the International Human Resources Committee. He is Chaplain of the Rochester NY chapter of his fraternity and was honored with their selection of him as their "Man of the Year" in 2004 and 2008. He is Coordinator of his fraternity's Omega Readers Program and was honored in 2012 by Wilson Commencement Park for ten years of service as a voluntary reader to Pre-K kids in their Early Learning Center. Joe has played a lead role in helping the fraternity's scholarship Foundation raise and donate more than a quarter of a million dollars to UNCF and other scholarship efforts in the Rochester, NY area.

Moreover, the International Grand Basileus of Omega Psi Phi Fraternity, Dr. Andrew Ray, and all the members of Joe's home chapter, Theta Omicron Chapter, showed their appreciation, respect, and love by honoring him in 2012 with the presentation of their "Citizen of the Year Award" for nearly 40 years of volunteer service to the Rochester, NY community.

Joe and Angie have been married for 41 years. They currently reside in Pittsford, NY, a suburb of Rochester, NY. They have three children and seven grandsons who live in Georgia and North Carolina who are intimately familiar with their Wilkes County history. Angie states, "When I first saw Joe, my spirit told me he was going to be my husband. We were only 14 years old at the time. We did not actually meet until we were 15. We married at age 23. Over the 41 years we have been married, I have found him to be everything I expected – loving, caring, disciplined, and committed to his family, his faith, his church, his careers, his fraternity, and his community. I am glad that he is my husband and the unsung hero of our family."

With his paternal grandfather, Deacon Roy Anderson having served at Reeves Chapel Baptist Church, his paternal great-grandfather, Deacon Wash Anderson having served at Mulberry Baptist Church, his maternal grandfather, Deacon Charlie Cofer having served at New Ford Baptist Church, and his maternal great-grandfather, Deacon Andrew Jackson Willis having served at Pole Branch Baptist Church, Deacon Joe L. Anderson, Sr. has also carried the family and Christian values of love, humility, commitment, hard work, and servant leadership into corporate America, academia, the military, and the larger society.

He states, "I give God the glory for all that He has done and continues to do with my life. He has brought me and my family a mighty long way. I am most grateful." We proudly claim this son of Wilkes County, Joe L. Anderson, Sr. as one of our Unsung Heroes.

PART FOUR

Military Leaders

"For God has not given us a spirit of fear, but of power and of love and of a sound mind."

2 Timothy 1:7

"Four score and seven years ago our fathers brought forth on this continent, a new nation, conceived in Liberty, and dedicated to the proposition that all men are created equal."

Gettysburg Address
November 19, 1863

"I credit most of my success to my family, a family that had expectations for the children of that family, for acquiring a fairly good education in the public school system and having a desire to get off the block."

General Colin Powell

Chapter 15

REVOLUTIONARY WAR SOLDIERS

African American soldiers have been heroes since colonial days (February 2011)

History tells us that between five and eight thousand enslaved and free Blacks valiantly served in the American (Continental) army during the Revolutionary War. In spite of the fact that the very first person to die in the war was a Black patriot named Crispus Attucks, George Washington and the Continental Congress did not decide to offer enlistment to Blacks until the British Royal governor of Virginia, Lord Dunsmore issued a proclamation offering freedom in exchange for service to indentured servants and enslaved Blacks.

In his book entitled, *An Imperfect God; George Washington, His Slaves, and the Creation of America,* nationally prominent historian and writer Henry Wiencek writes, "The men with Washington represented the hard core of devotion to the cause and to their commander. An astonishing number of them were Black." In July 1781 Washington's camp was visited by Baron Ludwig von Closen, an officer serving on the staff of the French Allies who surveyed the American army and wrote in his journal that "a quarter of them were Negroes, merry, confident and sturdy." Clearly, von Closen's professional evaluation was that "the Blacks were among the finest soldiers Washington had...."

This observation was further validated when Generals Washington and Lafayette hand-picked "the finest regiment in Washington's command" according to von Closen, the Rhode Island regiment, which was 75 percent Black, to carry out the most important assignment of the Revolution – the assault that ended the war – The Battle of Yorktown. In spite of their many sacrifices, their victory, and the triumph of the American Army in the Revolutionary War, the promised freedom for enslaved black patriots did not happen.

Many enslaved Virginians had served as substitutes for their slave masters with the promise that they would be freed after the war. Wiencek writes that "once independence was won, with their assistance, their masters managed to forget their promises and returned the men to slavery. The Virginia legislature passed a bill denouncing slave masters who contrary to principles of justice and to their own solemn promise" had failed to liberate those enslaved Blacks who had risked life and limb to free this country from British rule.

The desire to be free from the worst form of chattel slavery ever known to humankind burned deep in the hearts of the brave enslaved patriots, just as the desire today burns deep in the hearts of the brave young people of Tunisia, Jordan, and especially Egypt. The betrayal by the slave masters and the harsh realities of chattel slavery would prompt enslaved Blacks such as Gabriel

Prosser, Nat Turner, and Denmark Veasey to launch revolts to obtain freedom from slavery with as much courage as George Washington's quest for freedom from British rule.

Facing death for his part in the revolt, one of the enslaved patriots said "I have adventured my life in endeavoring to obtain the liberty of my countrymen, and am a willing sacrifice in their cause." Another, like Patrick Henry cried out, "Give me liberty or give me death." The yearning to be free is irrepressible. George Washington, Gabriel Prosser, Denmark Veasey, Nat Turner, Patrick Henry, Austin Dabney, and many others, including each of us, are witnesses to this phenomenon.

Author and attorney Michael Thurmond in his book entitled *Freedom* reminds us that Austin Dabney gained his freedom as a result of serving during the Revolutionary War as a substitute for his white master, and for his patriotism and exceptional bravery while helping to decisively defeat the British army in the Battle of Kettle Creek in Wilkes County. Former Georgia Governor and historian, George Gilmer states that "no soldier under Clarke was braver, or did a better service during the Revolutionary struggle" than Dabney.

Seriously wounded at Kettle Creek in February 1779, Dabney was taken to the nearby home of Lewis and Elizabeth Harris and their 13 year old son, Giles. During the long days of Dabney's recuperation, a bonding and personal relationship was formed with the family such that it was decided that Dabney would stay on after the wound healed. On January 30, 2010 more than twenty descendents of Lewis, Elizabeth and Giles Harris gathered in Pike County for the dedication of a new monument on the graves of Austin Dabney and William Austin Harris, and they shared the Harris Family story regarding Austin Dabney that has been passed down through the generations. They stated that over the ensuing

15 years after the Battle of Kettle Creek, Giles Harris and Austin Dabney worked together, collaborated in business transactions, and relocated from Wilkes County to Madison. They developed a special bond of friendship and mutual respect.

When a son was born to Giles and Elizabeth Harris, they named him William *Austin* Harris in honor of their friend Austin Dabney. Dabney assumed the role of mentor to Giles' son, William. He financially supported William while he was in law school and while he read the law with Judge Stephen Upson in preparation for the practice of law. Dabney was in the court room to celebrate with William when it was announced that he had passed the Georgia Bar exam. Dabney and William remained friends for life. When he died, Dabney left all his worldly possessions to William. William honored his friend and mentor by naming his son, Austin Dabney Harris. In his last wishes, William asked to be buried beside Dabney. The family complied.

The extraordinary heroic military service, life, and contributions of Austin Dabney compel us to regard him as an "**Unsung Hero of Wilkes County, GA.**" The State of Georgia would agree, even in 1786 and would grant him his freedom from slavery, land and a pension for his Revolutionary War service. He is most worthy of the decision by the City of Washington to erect a statue on the Square in his honor.

Chapter 16

AUSTIN DABNEY
(1765 - CIRCA 1830)

No soldier was braver than this distinguished loyal patriot (February, 2009)

During the period February 13-15, 2009, Wilkes County celebrates the victory by the Georgia Militia over the British military forces during the Revolutionary War (1775-1783) at the Battle of Kettle Creek. In the January 23 celebrative and informative kick off to this celebration in front of the Wilkes County Court House in Washington, local historian, Marion "Skeet" Willingham and others describe the 1780 founding of the city of Washington which was made possible, in part, by victory over the British at Kettle Creek on February 14, 1779.

Willingham points out that at the time of the Battle of Kettle Creek, only three Counties – Richmond, Burke and Wilkes remained under Continental Army control. Victory at Kettle Creek prevented Wilkes County and lands westward from going over to British control at that time.

In her article entitled, *Georgia's Black Revolutionary Patriot,* Carole E. Scott writes, "Just as was true with white Americans, black Americans fought on both sides during the Revolutionary War. Also true of both races was the fact that Tory (pro British) sentiment was strong in Georgia.

Helping convince many blacks to fight for the British was the fact that they were promised their freedom from slavery if they did so." Scott goes on to say that "after the war was lost by the British, some whites and blacks who had supported them were settled in Canada." The New Georgia Encyclopedia states that some were settled in Florida, the Bahamas, and Jamaica, as well. Scott adds that the number of black soldiers in both the British and American armies was limited by opposition to arming enslaved black men.

Phillip S. Foner in his book entitled, *History of Black Americans,* states that the number serving in the Continental (American) forces has been estimated at between 5,000 and 8,000 men. He goes on to say that "most blacks fighting for the American cause soldiered in the North. Georgian Austin Dabney was one of the few exceptions."

The Dictionary of Georgia Biography, Vol. 1, edited by Kenneth Coleman and Charles Stephen Gurr affirms that "Austin Dabney was a real person whose life can be documented through public records. According to his own statement, Dabney was born in Wake County, N. C. and came to Georgia by the late 1770s."

The Dictionary goes on to say that "He was a slave of Richard Aycock, who had moved to Georgia from N. C. and settled in Wilkes County. Aycock applied on behalf of Dabney for the latters bounty land in 1784. This was authorized for Dabney by Elijah Clarke because of Dabney's support of the patriot cause during the war. Aycock died shortly before 6 August 1786, in Wilkes County.

The following day, a committee of the Georgia House of Assembly was appointed to write a bill "'to emancipate and set free Austin, a mulatto fellow.'" "The law authorized Lieutenant Colonel Elijah Clarke and others to purchase Austin from Aycock's heirs for no more than seventy pounds sterling.

Once freed, he would be entitled by the recently passed state law to a state pension for a wounded or disabled soldier. Dabney was certified to receive a five-dollar-a-month state pension on 29 September. Later that state pension was converted into federal ones which he received until his death. Dabney lived in Wilkes County, Ga. from the time of his freedom until around 1804. It seems that he enjoyed the legal rights as a free person of color because he was involved in lawsuits there."

Carol E. Scott points out in her earlier referenced article that Dabney became a soldier in the Georgia Militia when his master, Richard Aycock avoided military service by presenting the enslaved Dabney as his substitute, a practice that Georgia and other colonies permitted. Michael Thurmond in his book entitled *Freedom,* points out that "Aycock circumvented the prohibition against slaves bearing arms by swearing that Dabney was a free person of color."

Thurmond goes on to say that "Out of necessity or indifference, military leaders apparently ignored Georgia's prohibition against enlisting black men, slave or free, in the militia." Thurmond adds that Dabney "distinguished himself as a brave and loyal patriot." Thurmond goes on to quote George Gilmer, an early Georgia governor and historian "No soldier under Clarke was braver, or did a better service during the revolutionary struggle." Thurmond adds that "In February 1779, Dabney fought in Georgia's bloodiest Revolutionary War battle at Kettle Creek, near the town of Washington in Wilkes County. The Georgia patriots won decisively, but Dabney was shot in the thigh and left seriously wounded on the battlefield.

Thurmond continues, "Giles Harris, a white Wilkes County resident, found Dabney, carried him to his house, and nursed him back to good health. For the rest of his life, Dabney worked to repay Harris for his kindness. To show his gratitude, the war hero became a laborer, friend, and benefactor to the Harris family. Dabney paid Harris' oldest son's (William)tuition at the University of Georgia, and arranged for the young graduate to receive his legal training in the office of a prominent Madison County attorney." Attorney William Harris would later name his son Austin Dabney Harris.

Michael Thurmond points out that "To assure Dabney would never be forced to bear the yoke of slavery again, the Georgia legislature passed a statute in 1776 officially granting the veteran patriot his freedom. ... The General Assembly accorded the war hero 'all the liberties and immunities of a free citizen...so far as free negroes and mulattos are allowed'. However, Dabney's military service and free status could not shield him from the pervasive anti-Negro bias that impacted every aspect of Georgia culture. Although his military service qualified him for a land pension, Dabney was denied the opportunity to participate in the 1819 state land lottery because of his race.

Two years later, the Georgia Legislature passed a special resolution granting Dabney 112 acres of land for his "bravery and fortitude." Angry white Madison County residents complained that it was an insult to white men for a former slave to be put on equality with them in the land distribution lottery. But Dabney enjoyed the support of several prominent white politicians, including Governor George Gilmer and Stephen Upson of Oglethorpe County, who introduced the legislation. The governor reminded the Madison Countians that Dabney had rendered "courageous service" during the Revolutionary War, and Gilmer chastised them for displaying what he described as 'unpatriotic' attitudes."

Thurmond hastens to add that "Dabney's contributions to the war effort were singular, but by no means unique. Several other black men served with distinction as combat troops in the patriot army. Nathan Fry joined Colonel Samuel Elbert's regiment at Savannah in 1775. Monday Floyd secured his freedom in 1782 by an act of the Georgia Assembly, which cited his heroic service during the war and directed public treasury to pay Floyd's owner one hundred guineas for his manumission. "

In addition, states Thurmond, "Georgia slaves made other important non-combat contributions to the patriot cause." "Slave labor became an increasingly important element in Georgia strategy as the war went on." Countless thousands of unnamed enslaved black people significantly contributed to the Revolutionary War effort. Unlike the authentic Black Revolutionary War hero, Austin Dabney, their names have been lost to history. But we are who we are because they lived and gave their all.

Chapter 17

JAMES, FRED & JOSEPH COFER

Cofer family active in military since World War I (February 2006)

Since the early part of the twentieth century there has been a descendent of Pope Cofer (1860-1930) and Fannie Standard Cofer (1866-1936) on active duty in the armed services. This tradition of military service has been honored in every generation of the Cofer family. In accordance with the national mandate set forth just prior to World War One that every able bodied man, age 18-45 register for the draft, their sons who were of age – Charlie, Jesse (Boykin), and Willie – signed up. Charlie Cofer had married Hattie Willis Cofer and they already had three children so he was not selected for active duty nor was Boykin. Willie Cofer was selected and served in combat overseas until the end of World War One.

Upon leaving the Army and becoming a farmer and deacon at New Ford Baptist Church, Deacon Willie Cofer, his brother Deacon Charlie Cofer and other deacons of the church negotiated with then School Superintendent W. T. Callaway, who had also served in the military, to enhance educational opportunities for New Ford students. This resulted in New Ford having the only African American church school in Northeast Wilkes County with grades 7-9 and with the only African American teacher in the black rural church schools who was a college graduate – Professor John Henry Jackson. Morehouse College graduate, Professor Jackson later went on to serve as principal of the Rosenwald School at Black Rock AME Church in Tignall, then to Washington High School in downtown Washington.

Both of Deacon Willie Cofer's sons, Lee Cofer and W. T. Cofer, served on active duty in the Army. Three of Deacon Charlie Cofer's sons served as well.

In his book entitled *History of Wilkes County,* Marion "Skeet" Willingham mentions one of these three, James Albert Cofer of Danburg, as one of the Wilkes County men who was decorated for heroism in combat (Bronze Star with "V" device) with the 93rd Infantry in the Pacific Theater.

James Albert Cofer
World War II – decorated for heroism in combat

A second son, Fred Cofer would serve first in the CCC Camp then in the Navy during World War II.

Fred Cofer
World War II

A few years later, their younger brother Joseph Cofer would serve in combat in Korea.

Joseph Cofer
Korean War

Several of Deacon Charlie Cofer's grandsons would serve in their generation. All three of James Albert Cofer's sons would wear a military uniform. The oldest, J. C. Cofer, would serve in the Air Force while Marion and George Cofer would serve in the Army during the Vietnam era. Other grandsons of Deacon Charlie Cofer would serve, as well. David "Sonny" Bland, Jr., son of David and Fannie Cofer Bland, was severely injured while serving as a Marine in Vietnam. His brother, Charles, would serve honorably in the Air Force. Luther Hanson, son of Walter and Sallie Cofer Hanson, would serve honorably in the Army.

Ed Anderson, Sr., son of Leroy and Veola Cofer Anderson, would serve in the Army for 21 years and would be decorated with a Bronze Star with "V" device for heroism in combat in Vietnam. After his retirement from the Army, Lieutenant Colonel Ed Anderson, Sr. would be enshrined in the Army ROTC Hall of Fame at his undergraduate alma mater, N.C. A&T State University. Ed's brother, Joe L. Anderson, Sr. would serve 2 active years in the Army and would retire as a Lieutenant Colonel from the Army Reserves after a total of 26 years. Lewis Heath, son of Walker and Lucy Cofer Heath and grandson of Deacon Charlie Cofer, would serve in the Air Force.

Deacon Charlie Cofer's great grandson, Jamal Cofer, son of J. C. Cofer and grandson of James Albert Cofer, would serve for several years in the Navy. Deacon Charlie Cofer's great grandson, Lewis K. Heath, Jr., son of Lewis K. Heath, Sr. and grandson of Walker and Lucy Cofer Heath, would serve in the Army. Deacon Charlie Cofer's great grandson, Tony Cofer, son of Cheryl Cofer and grandson of Fred Cofer, would serve in combat in Afghanistan with his army unit.

Deacon Willie Cofer's grandson, Dennis Cofer would serve honorably in the Marines, as would his grandson Roland Robinson during the Vietnam era.

The tradition of military service found in the Cofer family was very much alive in many other African American families as well. A visit to the cemetery of any African American church in Wilkes County reveals from the Veteran Administration headstones that a very large number of African American men throughout the history of Wilkes County and this nation have volunteered and honorably served their country. Beginning with Crispus Attucks, a Black man, and the first to die in the Revolutionary War, African Americans have served and many have given their lives for the freedoms we have in the United States of America.

The Cofer brothers, their sons, grandsons, nephews, and all other Wilkes County citizens who have dawned the uniform of our country are Unsung Heroes.

Chapter 18

COMMAND SERGEANT MAJOR SAMUEL EDWARD "ED" JENKINS

His many military citations, ribbons, and awards include the Silver Star (February, 2009)

Distinguished African American army career soldier, war hero, and civil servant, Command Sergeant Major (CSM) Samuel Edward "Ed" Jenkins was born April 1, 1934 in Wilkes County, Georgia to Frank C. Jenkins, Sr. (1908-1976) and Frankie Mae Porter Jenkins (1914-1962).

They operated a small store on Lexington Avenue where their children were taught responsibility, good work ethics, and loyalty to county and country. Frank, Sr. also operated a cab and was quite influential in the life of his children.

His sons have more than eighty years combined in the military. Ed insists that his parents strict discipline made serving in the military a very manageable career for him and his brothers.

Ed Jenkins' paternal grandparents were Anderson Jenkins, Jr. (1871- 1942) and Annie Anderson Jenkins. They were lifelong members of Hilliard Station Baptist Church. Anderson, Jr. was a surveyor and the owner of a saw mill. He exercised much influence in the life of Ed during his formative years.

Anderson Jenkins, Sr. and Ella Warren Jenkins are Ed Jenkins' paternal great-grandparents. Anderson Jenkins, Sr. migrated to Wilkes County from the Goshen area of Lincoln County after having fought in the Civil War. He decided to leave behind his former last name and he took on Jenkins as his new last name. He established himself in his new community as a farmer and God-fearing man who was one of the founding members of Flint Hill Baptist Church.

Henry Porter (1872-1928) and Bertha Murphy Porter are the maternal grandparents of Ed Jenkins and were lifelong members of Hilliard Station Baptist Church, as were the maternal great-grandparents of Ed Jenkins – Benjamin Murphy (? – 1941) and Polly Smith Murphy (1865-1944).

Other early influences in the life of Ed Jenkins were Emmie Lee Hill, a World War II veteran who had returned to Wilkes County after his service days and shared his adventurous stories with Ed and others. Miss Carrie Bell Stokes, a teacher, inspired and motivated him. Ed's experience as a young man delivering newspapers and milk, cutting grass, and working in his father's wood yard revealed to him the limitation of vocations in Wilkes County. To this day, he has much love for Wilkes County, but he realized early on, that he had to go elsewhere to experience a challenging career. After grades one through seven at Hilliard Station Elementary Church School and after high school at Washington Colored High School, he entered the US Army at Fort Jackson, South Carolina in 1951 at age 17 with the commitment to be a career soldier. He received 14 weeks of Basic and Advanced Individual Training at Schofield Barracks, Hawaii and reported immediately thereafter to serve in combat with the 24th Infantry of the 25th Division in Korea. He states that he spent much of his eighteenth birthday in a foxhole in Korea. He earned his first Combat Infantryman's Badge and other significant awards during this tour of duty.

Ed Jenkins was reassigned to support the Infantry School at Fort Benning, Georgia from 1952 through 1954 where he was promoted to the rank of Staff Sergeant. Then, he briefly experimented with civilian life for a few months. During that time he discovered that opportunities remained very limited in the South for him. He again enlisted and volunteered to return to Korea for service with Company "H", 7th Infantry Regiment as a Platoon Section Sergeant.

After completing his second tour of duty in Korea and earning the rank of Sergeant First Class, he was assigned to the 35th Infantry Regiment, 25th Infantry Division, Schofield Barracks, Hawaii. From 1957 through 1960, he was assigned to 7th Battalion, 2nd Regiment, Fort Jackson primarily as Platoon Sergeant and Mortar Instructor.

From 1960 until 1963 he enjoyed one of his more memorable assignments while serving with the 8th Infantry Division, Mannheim, Germany. In addition to the professional gratification he received while effectively serving as Platoon and Section Sergeant, 42 inch platoon, he and his family had the opportunity to grow through travelling all over Europe. They visited places others only read or dream about. Such places include England, France, Luxemburg, Berlin, and travel behind the iron curtain.

From 1963 through 1966, then SFC Ed Jenkins had the opportunity to serve his country as an instructor on the Basic Marksmanship Committee at Fort Gordon, which is only a stones' throw from his home town of Washington. Then, it was off to Viet Nam in 1967 and 1968 for combat service with Company "C", 1st Battalion (Mech), 5th Infantry, 25th Infantry Division, Chu Che, Viet Nam as Platoon and First Sergeant.

It was during this period of combat service that he earned his second Combat Infantry's Badge and the Purple Heart, because of injuries he received. But most importantly, he earned our nations' third highest award for heroism in combat during this assignment. The citation addressing the unselfish way in which he risked life and limb, appears later in this article. He returned to the United States in 1968 for service as First Sergeant, Company "B", 5th Battalion, 3rd Infantry, 6th Division, Fort Campbell, Kentucky.

In 1970, then First Sergeant received orders to serve at Fort Gordon. Later that year, he was assigned for the third time to Korea to serve as First Sergeant of Company "C", 1st Battalion, 32nd Infantry, 2nd Brigade, 7th Infantry Division, Camp Hovey, Korea. Upon his 1971 return to the states, he was assigned as First Sergeant, Company "A", 14th Battalion, 4th AIT Brigade, Fort Jackson, South Carolina. He received orders to report for his third assignment in Korea in 1974 for duty as First Sergeant, 2nd AG Company, 2nd Infantry Division, Camp Casey, Korea.

Of his nearly 27 years of honorably active duty, he served nearly one third of that time as a First Sergeant. When I inquired of him what the greatest highlight of his career was, he states that "it was the day I was promoted to First Sergeant." Clearly, he favored the high level of responsibility and total involvement with the mission and the troops that goes with being a First Sergeant. Moreover, others at high levels of the military recognized his superb service as a First Sergeant.

In January 1969, Major General S. H. Matheson had this to say about his service as a First Sergeant. "First Sergeant Jenkins distinguished himself by exceptional meritorious service from March 1968 through August 1968. As First Sergeant, Company B, 5th Battalion, 3d Infantry, Fort Campbell, Kentucky, First Sergeant Jenkins demonstrated the highest level of proficiency in the performance of his duties. Under his expert guidance and supervision, all his responsibilities consistently functioned in a smooth, efficient, and effective manner."

Later, when he received his second Army Commendation Medal for his outstanding service as a First Sergeant, the citation reads, "By direction of the Secretary of the Army, the Second Oak Leaf Cluster of the Army Commendation is awarded to First Sergeant Samuel E. Jenkins, US Army for meritorious service while serving as First Sergeant, Company E, 2nd Battalion, 1st Basic Combat Training Brigade, United States Army Training Center, Fort Gordon, Georgia, from 13 September 1968 to 6 January 1970.

During this period, First Sergeant Jenkins' performance of duty far surpassed that of normal standards. He consistently demonstrated outstanding professional competence, self-confidence, loyalty, initiative and determination. His vast knowledge, sound judgment, and ability to recognize potential problem areas for early corrective action contributed immeasurably to the effectiveness of Company E and the successful accomplishment of its mission.

First Sergeant Jenkins' loyalty, devotion to duty, leadership ability and efficiency marked him as an outstanding non-commissioned officer and earned him the respect and admiration of all with whom he came in contact."

The Citation for his third Army Commendation Medal reads thusly regarding his high level of competency when serving as a First Sergeant. "By direction of the Secretary of The Army, The Army Commendation Medal (Third Oak Leaf Cluster) is presented to Master Sergeant Samuel E. Jenkins for the period April 1971 to May 1974 for having distinguished himself by exceptional meritorious service and for the significant contribution he made to the United States Army Training Center and Fort Jackson, South Carolina, while serving as First Sergeant, Company A, 14th Battalion, 4th Advanced Individual Training Brigade (Combat Support). He consistently manifested exemplary professionalism and initiative and inspired others to achieve higher goals. Through his diligence and determination he invariably accomplished every task with dispatch and efficiency."

First Sergeant Jenkins was awarded a Meritorious Service Medal (MSM) for his outstanding service as a First Sergeant. His MSM Citation reads as follows, "First Sergeant Samuel E. Jenkins United States Army, distinguished himself by outstanding meritorious service as First Sergeant, company C, 1st Battalion, 32d Infantry, 7th US Infantry Division, from March 1970 to January 1971. During this period, First Sergeant Jenkins consistently demonstrated outstanding professional competence, loyalty and determination in fulfilling his duties. His skillful knowledge, aggressive action and sound judgment enabled his company to function as a highly effective unit."

Major General Hank "Gunfighter" Emerson sent a special and personal note on two-star stationary stating "I want to reiterate my congratulations on your selection for promotion to Sergeant Major. It is well deserved and serves as recognition of your contributions to the 'Second to None' and the army as a whole. I especially appreciate your fine work as First Sergeant in the Replacement Detachment. During your tenure great improvements have been made in both the processing of personnel and in the facilities for their use. This is especially important as the initial impression of PRO-LIFE received by the new arrival is based on your operation." Clearly Ed Jenkins was an exceptional First Sergeant who knew how to get the job done.

Upon being promoted to Sergeant Major, he served as Sergeant Major, Headquarters Committee Group, 1st Brigade, Fort Gordon from 1975 until 1978. His final assignment as Command Sergeant Major, 1st Battalion, 1st Signal Training Brigade, Fort Gordon, Georgia, was completed on 31 March 1978. Command Sergeant Major Jenkins retired from the US Army with 26 year, 9 months and 7 days of honorably active service.

Throughout his military career, Command Sergeant Major Jenkins received citations, ribbons, and other awards commending him for his outstanding performance of duty, whatever the assignment. His military awards include the Silver Star, the third highest award a soldier can receive for heroism in combat. More will be written about this coveted award later in this article.

Other awards he received include the Combat Infantryman's Badge (1st & 2nd awards), Bronze Star, Purple Heart with one Oak-Leaf Cluster (this means that Command Sergeant Major Jenkins was injured in combat on two separate occasions), Meritorious Service Medal with two Oak-Leaf Clusters, Air Medal, Army Commendation Medal with three Oak-Leaf Clusters, Korean

Service Medal with three Bronze Stars, Expatiation Medal, Vietnam Service Medal with two Bronze Stars, United Nations Service Medal, Vietnam Medal, Vietnam Cross of Gallantry with Palm, Korean Presidential Award, and many civilian awards and letters of commendation.

Few men and women in our nation's history have been awarded the Silver Star which is our nation's third highest award for heroism in combat. While conducting research for this article, I googled "Silver Star, Samuel E. Jenkins." I was elated that one of the references displayed was a page from the Congressional Record which is the official record of the proceedings and debates of the United States Congress. It is published daily when Congress is in session. Sure enough, there it was - a listing of CSM Samuel E. Jenkins along with many of our nation's heroes from the Korean conflict and VietNam as a recipient of the Silver Star.

These gallant men and women who fought in the Korean Conflict and The conflict in Viet Nam were at a year 2000 event in Washington, D. C. sponsored by a Veterans group. Among the host were Korean Conflict veterans – Congressman Charles Rangel of New York, now Chairman of the powerful House Ways and Means Committee and Congressman John Conyers of Michigan, now Chairman of the House Judiciary Committee, and Congressman William Clay of Missouri.

Further research reveals the following citation which was prepared in conjunction with the presentation of the Silver Star to Washington, Georgia's own Command Sergeant Major Samuel E. Jenkins.

Awarded by all branches of the Armed

Forces to any person who, while serving in action against an enemy of the United States while engaged in military operations involving conflict with an opposing foreign force.

Award: **Silver Star**
Date Action: 30 March 1967
Theater: Republic of Vietnam

Reason: For gallantry in action: Platoon Sergeant Jenkins distinguished himself by heroic actions on 30 March 1967, in the Republic of Vietnam. Company C was conducting a search and destroy operation near the Cambodian border and had been taken under intense enemy fire by a Viet Cong force of undetermined size. Almost immediately Sergeant Jenkins' armored personnel carrier, which was moving with the company command group, was struck by an enemy recoilless rifle round, seriously wounding Sergeant Jenkins and four of his comrades.

Though suffering severely from the shrapnel wounds he received, Sergeant Jenkins calmly and skillfully began organizing the command post group, directing a heavy volume of fire into the enemy positions. He fearlessly exposed himself to the withering small arms and recoilless rifle fire, continuing to direct his group's movement and arranging for the evacuation of the wounded personnel. Due largely to Sergeant Jenkins' inspiring leadership, the command post was able to suppress the enemy fire and force the insurgents to disperse.

Sergeant Jenkins then organized the command group and secured a landing zone for the medical evacuation of the wounded, refusing to board the helicopter himself until he was sure that all of his men were safely aboard. The undaunted spirit, personal fortitude, and devotion to duty displayed by Sergeant Jenkins are in keeping with the highest traditions of the military service and reflect great credit upon himself, his unit, and the United States Army.

Authority: By direction of the President under the provisions of the Act of Congress, approved 9 July 1918, and USARV message 16695, 1 July 1966.

Command Sergeant Major Samuel E. Jenkins is an authentic Wilkes County and American hero. When he was not in war or overseas , he was often in school. His military education includes: SEA Loading Course, Explosive Ordinance Recognition Course, Non-commissioned Officers Academy, 25th Infantry Division, CBR Detection and Contamination Course, Emergency Medical Care Course, Jungle Operations Course, Senior Non-Commissioned Officer and Staff Course, and Racial Awareness Course.

His civilian education includes an Associate of Arts in Business Administration, an Associate of Arts in Business Management and the Federal Law Enforcement Training Center Course.

Among his community activities, Ed Jenkins served as Scout Master of Boy Scout Troop, Augusta, GA; Past President of Old School Reunion Association, Washington, GA; Past Vice-President of the National 24th Infantry Regimental Combat Team Association, Inc.; Past Secretary of the National 24th Infantry Regimental Combat Team Association; Past President of the National 24th Infantry Regimental Combat Team Association; President of the Southeast Chapter of the National 24th Infantry Regimental Combat Team Association; Commander of Disabled American Veterans (DAV), Pendleton King Chapter 10, Augusta, GA, 2008-2009; Senior Vice Commander of Military Order of the Purple Heart – A. James Dyess Chapter 425, Augusta, GA, 2008-

2009.

Since his military retirement, he has completed a second career in Civil Service, advancing to the grade GS-12 during the period 1978 through 1996. The positions he held include Land and Residential Appraiser, Richmond County (1978-1980); Veterans Administration Hospital Staff, Augusta, Georgia (1980-1983); and U. S. Department of Energy Staff, Savannah River Site (1983-1996). As was the case with his military career, the bottom line of his civil service is "Job Well Done."

While he and his wife presently reside in Augusta, Georgia, Ed Jenkins has maintained his membership at Hilliard Station Baptist Church over the years. He regularly visits other churches throughout Wilkes and Richmond Counties, as well. His first wife, Vivian Willis Jenkins passed away in 1980 leaving him to be a single parent of three children, Vivian Rena Jenkins Oliver, Samuel E. Jenkins, Jr. and Frankie Lynn Jenkins Hubbard.

For the past nineteen years he and his wife, Diane B. Grant Jenkins have been happily united in holy matrimony. Together they parent six adult children and ten grandchildren. We pray that God grants continued long life, good health, prosperity, and Godspeed for this dynamic, authentic Wilkes County and American Unsung Hero and his family.

PART FIVE

Community & Family Leaders

"And we know that all things work together for good to those who love the Lord."

Roman 8:28

"If you can't fly then run, if you can't run then walk, if you can't walk then crawl, but whatever you do you have to keep moving forward."

Martin Luther King, Jr.

"There are two lasting bequests we can give our children. One is roots. The other is wings."

Hodding Carter, Jr.

Chapter 19

VEOLA "VEE" COFER ANDERSON

"Take the Lord with you everywhere you go"

She passed her zeal for education and the teachings of Jesus on to her children
(February, 2007)

We began our celebration of Black History month, 2007 by watching two good friends and Christian gentlemen become the first two African American coaches to coach in the Super Bowl. Because of the content of their character, their lifestyles, and their abilities, the lives of their players and coaches have been positively changed forever.

In a like manner, two Christian gentlemen of sound moral character, who were raised and nurtured in the Black church, attended the same college, and shared a philosophy that "education is the key to success" and "love one another" came together and infused their philosophies and spirit into the lives of young people who dared to seek an education at New Ford Church School, the only junior high school for Africans American students in the rural northeast sector of Wilkes County in the 1930s, 40s and early 50s.

The lives of the students they influenced and their descendants have been changed forever as a result of the character, example, and teachings of Rev. Albert T. Zellars and Professor John Henry Jackson, who were dominant influences in their lives. Veola Cofer Anderson is one of their successful students.

Born July 11, 1921 in Wilkes County, Georgia **VEOLA (VEE) COFER (ANDERSON)** is the fifth of eleven children born to Deacon Charlie Cofer, a farmer and Sister Hattie Willis Cofer, a homemaker. She attended the one room and one teacher Mulberry Church Elementary School during grades one through seven under the leadership of teacher and Principal Ella A. Glaze, as did most of her siblings. She had a natural and extremely strong desire for more education and the recently established junior high school at her home church, New Ford Baptist, would clearly fill her need.

Pastored by the highly spiritual and scholarly, Rev. A. T. Zellars, who was also pastor of Mulberry Baptist, New Ford Church and School was located approximately seven miles from the home of the Cofer family. Since they did not own a car, and her dad and older brothers could not take the time off from farming to get her to and from school, this appeared to be an insurmountable problem. But her father, who was a deacon at New Ford Baptist Church, understood both the educational yearnings of his daughter and the need to attract scholarly young students like Vee to New Ford Junior High School. He, after all had received a good basic education under Professor Bob Bradley at Bradleytown Elementary School, one of the first rural schools for African American students in Wilkes County.

The Christian way of helping one another back in those days enabled Deacon Cofer to call on another Christian family, Deacon Roy and Sister Ethel Willis Anderson, who he trusted to provide safe haven for his daughter while she waited at their home, after she and her 5 year old little brother, C. T. had walked two miles from the Cofer home to the Anderson home. From there they were picked up by Professor and Mrs. John Henry Jackson in his car and carried the remaining five miles to New Ford Junior High School.

The Anderson's daughter, Ethel Mae was also enrolled in the junior high school, as was Carrie Hudson (Gresham) (Mays), and the three of them became as sisters over a two to three year period as they daily came together to ride to school, study together in school, and ride back to the Anderson's home together. They benefited greatly from the wisdom and knowledge shared by Professor Jackson during those daily rides and they were enriched by his academic instruction in school.

Five year old C. T. Cofer, who was sent along by his parents to keep big sister Vee company as she walked the lonely two miles to and from the Anderson home, got an early start on his education since the first grade teacher, Mrs. Hattie Jackson, observed that he was very smart and could handle the curriculum of the early grades.

The Anderson and the Cofer families grew very close as a result of the arrangement for Vee. When she received her junior high school diploma, the county had not yet begun to provide bus transportation for African American students. Though rich in faith, values, and relationships, Vee's parents were farmers and had very little money, but she had high school and college very much in her plans and dreams.

She was absolutely heartbroken when it was determined that no satisfactory transportation or housing arrangements could be made for her to continue her schooling at Rosenwald School (16 mile round trip from her home to Tignall) or in Washington (20 miles round trip from her home). Everything appeared to be hopeless. She became a casualty of the nation's separate and unequal system of providing adequate education and transportation resources to white and not African American students.

In October 1943, she and the oldest son of Deacon Roy and Ethel Anderson, Leroy were married. They established and maintained a Christian home throughout their marriage. When Leroy went home to be with the Lord in July 2001, they had been married for 57 wonderful years and parented nine children. For the first ten years of their marriage, they were farmers. Then, in 1953, they moved to Charlotte N. C. and joined Ethel Mae Anderson Johnson who had earlier married Wade Johnson and moved there with their family. Leroy and Veola lived next door to Wade and Ethel Mae for the ensuing two years.

Even though they had five children by this time, Veola's thirst for education had not left her. She enrolled in and completed several correspondence courses after she finished caring for her home, husband and children at the end of each day. At the same time, she was persistently indoctrinating her children on the importance of education and spiritual growth. The teachings of Jesus, her parents, Rev. Zellars and Professor Jackson were being greatly emphasized in her home on a daily basis.

The oldest daughter of Leroy and Veola, Leola, had gotten off to a great start at the Rosenwald School (at Black Rock AME Church in Tignall, GA) prior to leaving Wilkes County. She was a very intelligent, determined, and poised child and, because she had mastered all the second grade material while she was still in the first grade, it was determined that she could be skipped from the first directly to the third grade. Leola and all her brothers and sisters went on to excel academically and to graduate from high school and college.

But Leola led the way and provided the role model which has been pursued by all her siblings and their children. She was the first to receive her mother's zeal for getting a good education and living a Christian life. She was always an "A" student throughout her years in school.

Leola was a member and president of the National Junior Honor Society in Junior High School and she graduated at the top of her class from high school and was on the National Honor Society. With a double major in English and French she graduated Magna Cum Laude from Johnson C. Smith University in 1966. She earned a Master of Arts Degree in Teaching English from Villanova University in 1979 and continued her studies at the University of Pennsylvania.

At the time of her untimely death from cancer at age 61 in January 2006, Leola had completed 39 years as a high school English and French teacher and Department Head and was the adult Sunday School teacher at her church. She was a member of

Alpha Kappa Mu Honor Society, Alpha Kappa Alpha Sorority and the National Council of Teachers of English. Leola's daughter, Nikki is following in her footsteps as a professional educator. Her son, James, Jr. is in the process of making a career change to the field of education.

Of Mama Vee's 9 children, three others are professional educators, two are Seminary educated ministers, one is an attorney, two are retired from corporate America and one is still in corporate America. Three of her five daughters are married to ministers or deacons and one is involved with lay ministry with The Gideons. All her sons are married to devout Christian women. Grandma Vee's emphasis on academic excellence and spiritual development is being passed down through the generations.

Of her 21 grandchildren, 18 are or soon will be college graduates. The remaining 3 are still grade school scholars, as are her 8 great grandchildren. Her grandchildren have or will soon graduate from the following colleges and universities – Howard University, University of Maryland, Georga Tech (2 graduates), Hampton, Morehouse, North Carolina A & T, North Carolina Central Univ (1 grad & 1 soon to be grad), Central Michigan, Univ of Miami, Florida International University (class of 2009), Duke (1 grad, set of triplets in the class of 2009), and Davidson (class of 2007). One of her grandsons is a 2nd year law student at the University of Miami.

All of the grandchildren are Christians and are fully aware of the source of their inspiration and achievement. They know the positive difference Grandma Vee has made in their lives and the lives of their parents. And they are becoming increasingly aware of the role of Rev. Zellars and Professor Jackson in her life.

Vee's good friend and schoolmate from childhood, Ethel Mae Anderson Johnson, obviously became her sister-in-law. The two of them are like sisters to this day. Both their husbands have passed, but their children and grandchildren are very active in their lives. By the way, two of Ethel Mae's daughter's are educators, as well. Daughter Deloris is a high school teacher and youngest daughter, Dr. Alice Johnson holds an earned Ph.D. and is a college professor. Daughter Pearl has a Masters Degree and is in corporate America. One son is deceased and the other, R. T. continues his career in management in the grocery store industry.

God's grace and the Christian home of Deacon Charlie and Sister Hattie Willis Cofer provided Vee with the foundation, core values and home training she needed to achieve great success in life. The lack of opportunity for education and advancement during the era of segregation and Jim Crow would not allow her to achieve her highest potential. But in His infinite wisdom, God enabled her to transfer her energy, zeal, intellect, love, the teachings of Jesus and her parents, and the teachings of Rev. Zellars and Professor John Henry Jackson to her children and grandchildren.

For her unselfishness and effectiveness in so doing, for her diligence, for her commitment to her family, for her love for God and all God's people, and for her constant encouragement of each of her children and grandchildren, she is indeed, an authentic unsung hero of Wilkes County, GA. and the world. Hers is an example of how one committed life can positively influence future generations. As people and as parents we can all learn much from her example.

Chapter 20

GARTRELL ROBINSON, JR.

Despite the hardships, he never lost hope (February, 2007)

Distinguished African-American career service member and Delta Airline mechanic, Gartrell Robinson, Jr. was born on July 12, 1930 at University Hospital in Augusta, Georgia, and was raised in the Danburg Community of Wilkes County by his uncle, Deacon Cap Robinson, a farmer, and his aunt Mrs. Daisy Robinson, a school teacher in the public/church schools of Lincoln County.

Both his parents passed away when he and his older brother, Marvin, were small children. He enjoyed his days as a student at New Ford Elementary School and was a quick learner but had to mix his schooling with farm work in the cotton fields. On the days he could attend school, farm chores had to be completed first, then a walk of more than two miles to get to school, followed by a day with grades one through seven compacted in only three small classrooms. Then there was a long walk home and more farm chores before doing homework and going to bed.

To this day Robinson is pained by his early recognition of the fact that school busses would pass him and his friends by as they made their long walks to and from school and would only stop and pick up his white playmates. He was aware that his school did not have new books or adequate supplies or facilities, but he knew that his teachers truly loved and cared for him and all their students and were working diligently to ensure that the students were properly educated and empowered to be successful and "be somebody."

Robinson's academic achievement and zeal for learning was such that it was determined that he be advanced from the 4th directly to the 6th grade. During his grade school years, it was determined through the negotiations of his Pastor, Albert T. Zellars, the New Ford Church deacons and trustees and the County Superintendent, that New Ford would offer a junior high school curriculum and diploma. This exciting news was amplified by the arrival of the new junior high and elementary school principal, Professor John Henry Jackson. At the time, Jackson was the only African American male teacher in Wilkes County with a college degree. Immediately, every young male student had a positive, high-achieving role model.

Needless to say, scholarly young Gartrell Robinson set his sights on college at the alma mater of Professor Jackson – Morehouse College in Atlanta, GA. He worked extremely hard to meet the stringent academic and disciplinary high expectations of Professor Jackson and all of his teachers. At the same time, he was determined to meet the even tougher expectations of doing his fair share of farm work set by his Uncle Cap. With faith in God, perseverance, and determination, he managed to keep all those in authority over him happy with his conduct and his academic performance.

Then came the upsetting news of the transfer of Professor Jackson from New Ford School to The Rosenwald School (at Black Rock Church) in Tignall, GA – some seven miles away. Gartrell's Aunt Daisy, who apparently had worked in the teaching profession in Lincoln County with Professor Jackson prior to his coming to New Ford, met with Jackson. Realizing that her nephew was greatly inspired and motivated to do his best work academically under the tutelage of Professor Jackson, she coordinated an agreement to get the very time-conscious Jackson to give her son a few extra minutes to walk, run, or otherwise travel seven or eight miles to Rosenwald each day in order to study under Jackson.

Robinson recalls the challenge of getting up very very early every morning, doing his farm chores, linking up with Howard Chennault, who was similarly inspired and motivated to get an education and to be mentored by Professor Jackson. They then had to make their way to Rosenwald School under all kinds of weather and road conditions. His grief with the county failing to provide bus transportation to African American students became more intense during the two years he had to struggle to get from Danburg to Rosenwald School in Tignall.

Sometimes road workers would pick him up, sometimes Robinson would jog much of the way, sometimes one of the white teachers from the Tignall High School, (believed to be the recently deceased school teacher, Mrs. Frances Duke) who seemed to respect and admire his thirst for education would give him a ride, especially on cold and rainy days. After years of dedication, hard work, sacrifice, and suffering, he earned his high school diploma in June of 1947. But his uncle's sharecropper wages had not been enough to put away any money for college. Plan B was to do three years in the Air Force, then enter college under the GI bill. The Korean War prolonged his military service.

Then came marriage to the love of his life, Mrs. Elizabeth Duren, a school teacher at New Ford School. (Theirs has been a long and happy marriage. They celebrated their 50th wedding anniversary in December 2006). With things going quite well for him in the Air Force, he opted to dedicate himself to a career in the military. Such a career afforded him the opportunity to be successful in a very challenging and rewarding career specialty which has had great transition value in civilian life.

Moreover, an Air Force career afforded him and his family the opportunity to live and travel and grow in environments far different from Wilkes County. Robinson was stationed in Korea, Alaska and Mississippi prior to being married. His family was with him while he was stationed in Illinois, California, Topeka and Wichita, Kansas. His most memorable assignments include his five years as a Bomber mechanic with the elite Strategic Air Command (SAC) in Kansas and as an instructor for aircraft mechanics in SAC and other units.

After military retirement in 1967 with the rank of Master Sargeant, Robinson transferred his aircraft mechanic skills to employment with Lockeed Aircraft, then to the City of Atlanta with duty as an aircraft mechanic at Hartsfield Airport. He has now completed a full career with the City of Atlanta and has retired and is finally relaxing a bit and enjoying spending time with his wife, children, and grandchildren in Atlanta, Georgia.

Four of their five children live in the Atlanta area. Like their dad and mom, they are bright and highly motivated. All of them are well educated and are in the middle of their careers. Daughter Andrea has a Masters Degree from Georgia Tech and is employed as a Procurement Officer. Son Hollis is a graduate of S. C. State University and works for Westinghouse as a Sales Manager. Daughter Henrietta works as a civilian contractor at Fort

McPherson, GA. Son Mayce works as a mechanic. Son Gartrell, the 3d lives in Dallas, Texas and is in the Security business.

Gartrell Robinson continues to serve as an active member of New Ford Baptist Church. Since New Ford has traditionally met only on the 4th Sunday each month until recently, he and his wife are active members of Shaw Temple in Smyrna, GA, as well. His quest for success all started with the care and inspiration of his Uncle Cap and Aunt Daisy, and was nourished and propelled by the guidance, inspiration and motivation of Professor John Henry Jackson and Rev. Albert Zellars. Mr. and Mrs. Gartrell Robinson, Jr. have passed on their quest for academic and spiritual excellence to their children and grandchildren who have received the torch and are doing quite well.

Despite the hardships, Gartrell Robinson never lost hope. He persevered and he, his wife and family overcame the oppression of Jim Crowism. He is unquestionably an Unsung Hero of Wilkes County, Georgia.

PART SIX

Government/Law Enforcement Leaders

"Trust in the Lord with all your heart, and lean not on your own understanding; in all thy ways acknowledge Him, and He shall direct thy paths."

Proverbs 3:5-6

"There was something of a tradition of hard work being the way to succeed. And there was simply an expectation that existed in the family – you were supposed to do better. And it was a bloody disappointment to the family if you didn't."

General Colin Powell

"All that is necessary for evil to flourish is for good men to do nothing."

Edmund Burke

CHAPTER 21

WILLIE C. BOLTON

Through perseverance, he prepared for opportunity (February, 2011)

Distinguished African American Warden/Director of the Department of Corrections for Athens-Clarke County Georgia, Willie C. (W.C.) Bolton was born in 1950 in Rayle, Georgia to Claude Bolton, a construction worker, and Daisy Harden Bolton, a strong mom and homemaker who in her later years joined the workforce and rose to the level of supervisor on her job.

He credits them with instilling in him pride in the Bolton name and other time honored values that have enabled him to be successful in life. Having begun school before desegregation, he first attended White Rock Baptist Church School, a one room school with one teacher teaching grades one through six.

The following year, all Wilkes County church schools for black students were closed and most black students were required to attend Wilkes County Training School.

While there, he was influenced by many excellent teachers who were positive role models and parent figures, as well. They included shop teacher-Mr. Isaac Stevens, "dean of boys"-Mr. Charles Reid and math teacher-Ms. Essie Bell. Long after his graduation, he and Mr. Reid (affectionately called "Big Reid") were good friends. The wisdom and words of Ms. Bell still provide counsel to him in many life situations.

Even now, when things get tough he remembers her saying, "Life isn't fair, if it knocks you down, you don't have to stay down; get up, dust yourself off, and keep on going." Her constant reminder to "be prepared" to take advantage of new opportunities is his philosophy as well, and he regularly shares this same advice with family and friends.

After graduating from Washington Central High School in 1968, Warden Bolton served as an apprentice electrician with a construction company and then worked for Westinghouse. In 1973, Athens, Georgia experienced two major tornados. Law enforcement officers were exhausted from working to keep traffic flowing. He observed a very tired law enforcement officer directing traffic, so he offered to assist him. The grateful officer complimented him on his helpfulness and professionalism, and invited him to put his talent to work by applying for a job with the Sheriff's Office.

After discussing the offer with his wife, LuNeal, he accepted the opportunity. At the time of his hiring by Sheriff H. T. Huff, he was asked to consider undertaking at least a twenty-year career in law enforcement. More than thirty-seven years later, he has served in many meaningful and challenging positions while working his way up through the ranks. In 1994, he was appointed Warden/Director by the Unified Government of Athens-Clarke County and he currently serves in that position.

While not college prep oriented during his high school days, his desire to heed the words of his former teacher, Ms. Essie Bell and "be prepared for opportunity", and the advice of mentors in the Sheriff's Department have inspired him to constantly grow, improve, and be the best possible law enforcement officer.

As a result, he has earned an undergraduate Criminal Justice degree from Brenau University and a graduate degree in Public Administration from Clark Atlanta University. He has also earned a Georgia Public Safety Executive Certification. His quest for self improvement and preparation for opportunity has been a pathway to his present position. Along the way he has established lifelong relationships with police chiefs and other law enforcement officers throughout the nation.

Moreover, he has been called on to serve his profession in leadership positions in law enforcement professional organizations such as The Georgia Prison Warden Association, GA Peace Officers Standards and Training Council (POST), and NE Georgia Police Academy. A strongly civic and community minded man, he has unselfishly served in leadership positions in NE Georgia Council of Boy Scouts of America, Athens Rotary Club, Athens Regional Medical Center and most importantly, his church.

A lifelong member of White Rock Baptist Church, he was ordained a deacon before he was thirty years old. He and his family also now worship and serve at Athens East Friendship Baptist Church where they are members, as well.

Director Bolton's commitment to the teachings of scripture has always been a guiding force in his personal and professional life. He is concerned that many of the young inmates, under the age of twenty-five who are confined at his correctional facility are unchurched. Through prison ministry programs available to them, many are inspired to change their lives.

Director Bolton issues a challenge to ministers and other religious leaders in our county to expand church outreach programs and make greater efforts to touch the lives of our young people before they are introduced into the criminal justice system. He is passionate about encouraging greater commitment to parenting, mentoring, and community building by adults to facilitate the tough loving village it takes to raise a healthy, law abiding, self-respecting child, who can and must be the hope of our future.

Director Bolton's personal and professional service to the Clarke and Wilkes County communities has been recognized with awards from the NAACP, Rotary Club, Cedar Shoals High School, the Secretary of States' Office and many others. He has been awarded the "Key to the City" of Athens by two different mayors and he has served in various capacities with four governors of Georgia.

His aspirations are to serve for years to come. His former teacher Ms. Bell, has given him reason to believe that his calling, at a future time, includes service to the people of Georgia in political office. Until he hears from her again, he desires that each of us reach out each day and build our communities, support and hold accountable our elected officials, and extend a helping hand to someone or some meaningful cause each day of our lives.

Because of his service to community, church, and profession, his caring commitment to his family, staff and fellow citizens, and the quality of his character, Willie C. Bolton is a genuine "unsung hero of Wilkes County, GA."

PART SEVEN

Civic Leaders

"I can do all things through Christ who strengthens me."
Philippians 4:13

"The best years of your life are the ones in which you decide your problems are your own. You do not blame them on your mother, the ecology, or the president. You realize that you control your own destiny."
Albert Ellis

"The person who really wants to do something finds a way; the other person finds an excuse."
Author Unknown

Chapter 22

REESE J. BOOKER

A life committed to education, growth, and development (February, 2008)

Distinguished African American educator and community leader, Reese Jack Booker was born around 1918 in the Pento District of Wilkes County Georgia. The 1930 Census reflects that his 45 year old mother Sallie Lou Booker was the head of the household and was parenting three children - twelve year old son, Reese Booker, fourteen year old daughter, Clara Booker, and ten year old son, O. D. Booker.

The census records show that his mother was a farmer and that each child was a farm laborer. Raised with a determined work ethic, Reese Booker worked many odd jobs while in high school, among them were serving as a caddy at the local golf course, being a janitor, and working as a fruit picker.

Gibson Grove Baptist Church was the family church and was significant in the spiritual development of all the Booker children. After completing high school in Washington, Georgia, Reese Booker enlisted in the Navy where he served honorably as a cook for several years. Having been positively influenced in Wilkes County by the local Black Presbyterian minister and educator Rev. William Woods, Reese Booker, upon being honorably discharged from the Navy, used his hard-earned GI Bill educational benefits to prepare himself for a career as a teacher by attending Tuskegee Institute (now Tuskegee University) in Tuskegee, Alabama, which specialized in preparing black people to be teachers and leaders in their communities.

Tuskegee Institute was originally led by Booker T. Washington who once visited Washington, Georgia during the early part of the 20th century as a guest of Dr. Frederick Douglas Sessoms, I'm told. He was probably positively influenced by Tuskegee's second president, Robert Moton, who served after the death of Dr. Booker T. Washington in 1915 until 1943.

Undoubtedly he was also influenced by one of the most outstanding scientist of the era, Dr. George Washington Carver, who served on the faculty at that time. These giants in the field of education and other Tuskegee faculty and staff aggressively met the challenge of molding and shaping young men to be strong educational leaders in their school systems.

Reese J. Booker began his career as an educator in Wilkes County at New Salem Baptist Church School back during the era of segregation. Later, he taught at the elementary school in Tignall. Lastly, he taught at Wilkes County Training School/Washington Central High School. According to retired educator, Deacon Eddie Finnell, "he committed his life to the education, growth, and development of his students and the children of Wilkes County, Georgia. Mr. Booker set a superb example for the young men he worked with. He did not smoke, drink or use profanity." He never married or had any children of his own.

Deacon Finnell further shares that Mr. Booker established a Boys Club in the school for the young male students. Later he established a Boy Scout Troop, as well." He purchased a new car every three years and would use it to transport his ball teams (no reimbursement was made by the school system), scouts and boys club to colleges to inspire them; to the nations capital, Philadelphia, PA; and to other significant historical and cultural sites." With his own money, he purchased a radio for his students to listen to current events, specifically the Paul Harvey News.

Retired educator, Ms. Clara Sutton, states that he was her seventh grade math teacher and "he knew his subject and how to make it interesting to his students." She goes on to say that "he would often provide incentives to students to correctly do their math problems." He was called on by his school principal, Professor John Henry Jackson, to serve as disciplinarian and as coach of several different sports teams including the superb boys basketball team. His academic, coaching, and disciplinary skills cause him to be well remembered by his former students to this day.

During non-school hours, Mr. Booker could be found on Whitehall Street at the playground that bears his name. In fact, he established residence in a mobile home on the playground. He took the initiative to procure the playground land, establish the playground, obtain necessary equipment, lay out ball fields, and manage and supervise the young people who would regularly use the playground.

This was the only organized recreational facility for African American young people in town, and equipping and operating it was a ministry to Mr. Booker. On that playground he set up a softball field, a basketball court, a skating rink, a miniature golf course, a swing area, a merry-go-round and see-saw area, a concession building, and an equipment storage area. He took full responsibility for running the playground year round and for maintaining it by keeping the grass cut and keeping everything else in order.

Mr. Booker maintained good relations with then mayor, Mr. Ed Pope, and the city council which enabled him to procure some features for the playground. In fact, it is said that Mr. Booker was a genuine Christian who maintained good relations with everyone.

A few years after moving his membership to Marks Tabernacle Baptist Church, Mr. Booker was ordained a deacon and he was elected to the position of Sunday School Superintendent. Many of the students he taught during the week were his students in Sunday School, as well. Historic Springfield Baptist Church had a different meeting day than Marks Tabernacle which enabled Mr. Booker to worship, teach Sunday School, and otherwise serve at Springfield, as well.

Mr. Booker poured his life into the lives of so many young students in Wilkes County especially the young male students who may not have had an active father in the home. They responded with appreciation, respect, hard work, and a commitment to make something of their lives. When asked what she knew about Reese Booker, funeral home director, Mrs. Bessie McLendon stated that "he genuinely cared about his people."

Nephew Jimmy Booker of Atlanta who was raised by Reese Booker has nothing but love, respect, and admiration for his Uncle

Reese who raised him after his mother , Clara, passed away. He stated that "he is the reason for any success I have enjoyed in life." Jimmy especially recalls being in the Boy Scout Troop organized by Scoutmaster Reese Booker and having to learn the Scout Law, Scout Oath, and Motto.

He has fond memories of the many overnight camping experiences in Harlem, Georgia and elsewhere, the annual Jamborees, and the many parades the scouts marched in as a drill team. Niece Clara Booker of New York says that "Uncle Reese always liked to help people. He was always there when I needed him." "He really wanted everybody to just do the right thing."

Indeed, Mr. Booker made a very positive difference in the lives of so many young people of Washington and Wilkes County in the school system, in the churches, in the community, and on the athletic field. Every six months, Sister Clara Sutton puts on a program at Marks Tabernacle Baptist Church designed to raise money to be presented to deserving college students. She has named that scholarship fund the Reese J. Booker – Rosa Warthen Scholarship Fund.

Many college students from Wilkes County have received scholarship money from that fund. This is a real tribute to the life and service of Mr. Booker. Moreover, the recreational area he established, operated and maintained is now named Reese J. Booker Park Youth Center and is located on Reese J. Booker Ave. The current city administration, under the leadership of Mayor Willie Burns has contributed significantly to the upkeep of the Reese J. Booker Recreational Area.

African American men and others in the community must take note of the life and service of Reese J. Booker. Many sons of Wilkes County need a Reese J. Booker in their lives. Our challenge is to step up to the plate and, like Mr. Booker, be a father to every young man in our neighborhood. We must teach them, guide them, spend time with them, discipline them. Now is the time to *turn the hearts of the fathers to the sons.*

Thank you Mr. Reese J. Booker for a life well spent. Thank you for your example. You are an authentic Unsung Hero of Wilkes County, Georgia.

ABOUT THE AUTHOR

Edward M. Anderson. Sr.

A native of Wilkes County, Georgia, Ed Anderson, Sr. was educated in the public schools of Wilkes County and Charlotte-Mecklenburg County, N.C. He is a Distinguished Military Graduate of North Carolina A&T State University with a Bachelor of Science degree in Economics. He is a law school graduate and a licensed attorney who is a retired Lieutenant Colonel from the U.S. Army JAG Corps. Additionally, he is a seminary graduate and an ordained Baptist minister who serves as Assistant Pastor in his church. Moreover, he is "all but dissertation" on his Ed. D., and is a retired public and Christian school educator. Presently, he serves as a part-time Municipal Court Judge.

Website address:
http://www.andersonministriesofwilkescounty.com

EPILOGUE

The entire generation of those who are called Unsung Heroes in this publication, endured a tremendous amount of pain, anguish, disappointment, and heartache. But, by and large, they kept the faith, they persevered, and they worked hard and prayed hard for a better day for their children and children's children.

In the veins of many of these Unsung Heroes of Wilkes County flow the blood of Native Americans, Africans, and Europeans. Their history, though much of it is not written, is rich and deep. Many of their ancestors arrived in Georgia from Virginia, North Carolina, and other colonies with the white settlers and they contributed greatly to the building of our civilization. They toiled under the horrific yoke of slavery and oppression.

These Unsung Heroes, their ancestors, and descendants fought with great sacrifice in the Revolutionary War, the Indian Wars, the War of 1812, the Civil War, the Spanish-American War, World War I, World War II, the Korean Conflict, the Vietnam Conflict, the Gulf War, the Bosnian Conflict, the Iraq War, the War in Afghanistan, and other conflicts. They fought valiantly, bled, and even died to protect a way of life that they often could not fully enjoy.

Many of our Unsung Heroes and/or their children had to migrate from Wilkes County in order to achieve their highest potential. They, and the vast majority of their descendants continue to work to uplift God, country, and family and they continue to stand on **the promises of God**:

"The LORD is my Shepherd, I shall not want." Psalm 23:1

"… I will never leave you, nor forsake you." Hebrews 13:5

"And the LORD said, I have surely seen the affliction of my people who are in Egypt, and have heard their cry by reason of their taskmasters: for I know their sorrows." Exodus 3:7

"Many are the afflictions of the righteous, but the LORD delivers him out of them all." Psalm 42:11

"God is our refuge and our strength, a very present help in times of trouble." Psalm 46:1

"Behold God will not cast away the blameless, nor will He uphold the evil doers." Job 8:20

"Finally, my brethren, be strong in the LORD and in the power of His might. Put on the whole armor of God, that you may be able to stand against the wiles of the devil. Above all, taking the shield of faith with which you will be able to quench all the fiery darts of the wicked one. For we wrestle not against flesh and blood, but against principalities, against powers, against the rulers of darkness of this world, against spiritual wickedness in high places." Ephesians 6:10-12

"For God so loved the world, that he gave His only begotten Son, that whosoever believes in Him shall nor perish, but have everlasting life." John 3:16

BIBLIOGRAPHY

Monument

Village of Danburg Granite Memorial. Danburg, GA – Corner of Bradford Road & Highway 44.

Books

The Original African Heritage Study Bible (KJV). Nashville, TN: The James C. Winston Publishing Co., 1993.

Anderson, James D., *The Education of Blacks in the South, 1860-1935.*Chapel Hill and London: The University of North Carolina Press, 1988.

Bartlett, John. *Familiar Quotations.* Boston, MA: Little, Brown and Co., Inc., 14th Edition, 1968.

Brokaw, Tom. *The Greatest Generation.* New York, NY: Random House, Inc., 1998.

Coleman, Kenneth and Durr, Charles. *Dictionary of Georgia Biography, Vol. 1.* Athens, GA: University of Georgia Press, 1983.

DuBois, W. E. B. *Black Reconstruction in America, 1860-1880,* New York. Simon & Schuster, 1995.

DuBois. W. E. B. *The Negro Church.* New York, Oxford. Alta Mira Press, 1903.

Evans, Cecelia Gartrell. *Appointed to Tell. A Chronicle of Springfield Baptist Church.*
Media, Pennsylvania: Cecelia Gartrell Evans, 2000.

Evans, Cecelia Gartrell. *Appointed to Tell More. A Chronicle of Springfield Baptist Church (org. 1868) and Rev. Lewis Williams 1821-1906 of Washington-Wilkes County, GA.*
Media, Pennsylvania: Cecelia Gartrell Evans, 2001.

Finnell, Kay. *Education in Wilkes County, GA from 1922 to 1970.* Washngton, GA: Wilkes Publishing Co., 2003.

Neyland, James. *Crispus Attucks, Patriot.* New York, NY: Kensington Publishing Corporation, 2008.

Saggus, Charles Danforth. *Agrarian Aracadia – Anglo Virginian Planters of Wilkes County, Georgia in the 1850's.* Washington, Georgia: Mary Willis Library, 1996.

Sernett, Milton C. *African American Religious History-A Documentary Witness.* Durham, N. C.: Duke University Press, 1985.

Stephens, Ray B. *Minutes of Danburg Baptist (Formerly Newford Baptist), Wilkes County, Georgia.* Chamblee, Georgia: Georgia Department of Archives and History, 1973.

Thurmond, Michael. *Freedom.* Atlanta, GA: Longstreet Press, Inc., 2003.

The Washington-Wilkes Historical Foundation. *Heritage of Wilkes County, Georgia - 2010,* Washington, GA: Washington-Wilkes Historical Foundation, 2010.

Wiencek, Henry. *An Imperfect God. George Washington, His Slaves, and the Creation of America.* New York, NY: Farrar, Straus, and Giroux, 2003.

Willingham, Jr., Robert M. *The History of Wilkes County, Georgia.* Washington, GA: Wilkes Publishing Co., 2007.

Thesis/Dissertation

Saggus, Charles Danforth. "A Social and Economic History of the Danburg Community in Wilkes County, Georgia." M.A. thesis, University of Georgia, 1951.

West, Jennifer Boone. "Before We Reach the Heavenly Fields: Religion and Society in Wilkes County, Georgia – 1783-1871." Ph.D. dissertation: Emory University, 1995.

Newspapers

The News-Reporter, Washington, GA

Interviews – 1970's

J. P. Cofer
Sallie Cofer Hanson
Fannie Cofer Bland
James Albert Cofer
Fred Cofer
Dea. & Mrs. Roy Anderson
Dea. & Mrs. Charlie Cofer
Lillian Willis Andrews
John Major

Interviews – 1980's

Ethel Mae Anderson Johnson
Carrie Hudson Mays
Mary Sale Stennett
David Sale
Joseph Cofer

Interviews – 1990's

Dr. Charles D. Saggus

Interviews – 2000's

Rev. Kenneth Walker
Oree Dee Willis
William James Willis
Dorothy Sprowl Willis
Jimmy Willis
Geri Willis Pero
Mary Lee Suttles
Minnie Ruth Marsh
Jimmy Booker
Clara Booker
Clara Sutton
Eddie Finnell
Kay Finnell
CSM "Ed" Jenkins
C. T. Cofer
Dea. & Mrs. Albert Rucker
Dea. & Mrs. D. W. Dunn
Rev. & Mrs. H. M. Easley
Rev. Albert Huyck
John Jackson
Booker Jackson
Charles Jackson
Andrew Jackson
Bessie McLendon

Interviews – 2010's

Chancellor Harold Martin
Arthur "Doc" Danner
Reber Neal
Mike Eskew
Leola Anderson Young

Dea. & Mrs. Joe L. Anderson
Rev. William Thomas
Former Mayor, Willie Burns
Mrs. Addie Burns
CSM Roy L. Burns, Jr.
Lynn Burns
Nedra Burns
David Burns
Daniel Burns
Anita Burns

Made in the USA
Charleston, SC
12 July 2014